Women Behaving Badly
Alana Munro

Contents

Acknowledgements

This book is dedicated to my husband, Michael.

Thank you for teaching me the importance of compromise, tolerance and loyalty.

To our beautiful sons,

Ethan, Arden and Laike,

Who have taught me how to love and what truly matters in life.

I hope our boys can learn from the ridiculous mistakes I have made with women and I hope they can learn lessons from the misery and pain I have personally endured.

And to my dear grandmother, Alice, who sadly died whilst I wrote this book.

I miss the endless head, leg and foot massages you gave me, the midnight feasts we would enjoy together during sleepovers, the postage stamps you always had in the kitchen cabinet for me to claim, the all-day shopping trips to Edinburgh where you spoiled me silly, the creative cakes that you baked for my birthdays, the oranges that you cut up beautifully for me whenever I asked – carved into beautiful baskets and sprinkled with sugar no less, the stale smell of your cigarettes and most of all your feisty and passionate character. You were everything a girl could have hoped for and more.

Introduction

"This is my last day. I'm leaving. This shop doesn't pay near enough." Lisa, a striking woman in her late twenties, sighs as she fills in my order form. *"How's Monday for delivery?"*

I smile and nod, *"Yup, sounds perfect, thanks. So where are you going to work?"* I ask casually.

She scans my face for a whiff of judgment. Pleased to see I am simply interested, she smiles sweetly before whispering, *"Anywhere that has more men. I need a ratio of more men to women. That's the secret to happiness in work, well in life, too."*

"Really?" I gently probe. Inside, deep within my very core, I sigh.

I already know what she is implying. I already know her reality, but I'm eager for Lisa to speak it. Guiltily, I want to hear the truth pour from another woman's glossy red lips. I want the validation that another woman out there also has problems relating to females. I want to feel reassured that I am not alone in this very personal struggle with women.

How shamefully indulgent of me, please forgive me, but once you read my personal struggles, perhaps you will then understand my need for this stranger's declaration. Perhaps you will come to understand the desire I hold in my heart for solace. I'm standing there before a stranger and I'm secretly hoping that her words will bring some much needed comfort to my weary disposition.

Lisa's hushed tones, and her narrow eyes that dart across the room, say it all - this is dangerous territory. We must be careful no one hears. This heavy secret, our feminine reality that women frequently struggle with one another, cannot be exposed. The bitter truth that women can be absurdly cruel to other women.

Why is this risky conversation social suicide? Why the whispering?

Men will only belittle our female power struggles. *"Women causing drama and falling out as usual over stupid crap,"* the men smirk to one another at the water cooler.

If women hear, they may shun us. They might take offence or judge us. They might join in.

Either way, no one really wins in the battle *between* women. Men think we are hysterical and take things too personally. Women think we can't be trusted (resulting in tense and guarded exchanges) or they jump on board and seize the opportunity to bitch about another woman, further spreading the negativity.

Lisa knows this. I know this. From experience, women learn tough lessons. We learn to be cautious or we learn early to join in - *bitch or be bitched about.* It's unclear who we can trust.

We long for the closeness and softness of a sweet natured woman, but with women, we know it is risky. We learn that women are harder to please. It is harder to emotionally satisfy a woman. We also learn that women tend to hold grudges and can make our daily life quite unbearable if they want to.

Careful not to attract attention, Lisa pauses and then she looks up at me rather apprehensively and offers, *"If I have a problem at work, I tell John and ten minutes later we are cool. It's forgotten. If I tell a woman what's wrong, ten months later she is still pissed off with me."*

"They just won't let it drop?" I encourage.

"Yeah. Exactly. They just won't let it go. It's mentally exhausting. With women, I don't know if they like me or want to boil my head. They pretend everything's cool, but they are furious inside. She smiles at me, eats her lunch with me, but I know she is just tolerating me. She just can't move forward."

Of course, I know that men can and do display similar behaviours. Men are no stranger to mind games, manipulation and bullying. But there's a wounded girl in me and she can't help but nod along in agreement with Lisa.

I recognise Lisa's struggles. I also know it is almost impossible to know what a woman is thinking. She is hugging you or smiling at you, but her feelings about you may be very different. However, with men, you generally know if they like you or want to smash your skull in. Women *try* to disguise their negative feelings (of course, the anger floods out in other ways!). Men find it more of a struggle to hide their anger or they see no need to hide their negative feelings.

Lisa won't be the first woman to be on the lookout for a mostly male work force. And I have to admit her strategy does sound rather appealing, however, no doubt, rather flawed. But who am I to argue with Lisa, the footie chit chat is less emotionally rewarding, but at least it is safe. I guess when a girl's been badly burnt by other women, she longs for a benign, easy environment.

After this unexpected encounter with Lisa, I can't stop thinking about her. Her hushed tones. Her desperation to escape the emotional minefield that can be females. Inside she was screaming, but outside she was calm, restrained and smiling. It was astonishing. It saddened me. It was all too familiar. I had been Lisa.

Many times - *too* many times.

And then it comes to me.

Lisa was young, slim, pretty, blond, clever, outspoken and confident. She was everything a woman would like to be. Or perhaps Lisa was everything society believes a woman should be. It becomes transparent why someone who is like Lisa would have had issues with females all through her life.

But surely it can't be so simple?

It seems preposterous that women would seek to make Lisa's life more complicated because she is a size 10, has beautiful hair or she seems to have it all, according to the strict social norms of womanhood.

I dig a little digger.

***

"Oh yeah, men are easier. I prefer to hang out with blokes," my beautifully candid friend, Sara, says over a coffee.

I tease, *"But you hang out with me and I have a vagina?"*

"Uh, you're different, not like most, more like a bloke." She hits my leg and smiles.

Is it a compliment to be *more* like a bloke? I don't know if I should be flattered or not, but I push on; I can't help but delve.

"Alright, so why do you think that, Sara?"

"Oh, come on, you know, Alana!"

"I know, yes, I know, but I want you to tell me your thoughts."

She goes on, *"Women are just so complicated. I can't seem to navigate relationships with women. It always seems to end in disaster! You know what? I'm glad I'm not a lesbian. I'd be crap at keeping a girl!"*

I smile.

She looks at me and apprehensively sips her coffee. This is good, *really* good information. I gently squeeze her for more.

"Go on. Tell me why? I'm all ears."

Sara blurts out, *"I can't seem to maintain a healthy relationship. It seems too hard to balance. The expectations can be huge. There is usually an undertone, things not being said. Things fester. Before you know it, one of you, or both of you, are bitching about the other over some ridiculously stupid complaint, something she didn't do right or something insensitive that she said weeks ago. We just can't accept each other's flaws. We all think we are perfect friends and that's a big problem!"*

I concur. *"More coffee?"*

The Fight to Write This Book

I think I prefer the way men conduct their relationships with their male friends. Why do I say this? I believe that males are *in general* fairer on their own kind.

Women are unfair on each other and women are often unfairly critical of themselves.

We are harsh on ourselves and often just as harsh on other women.

Women, who struggle to be fair and struggle to love themselves, will struggle to play fair and love *other* women.

It's an important question to consider.

How can we women be emotionally generous to other women if we struggle with the concept of respecting *who we are*?

Men, in contrast, seem to have an easier ride with their friendships. I couldn't ignore these inherent differences. There was little doubt in my mind that women conduct their friendships differently from men. It was time to probe deeper. I wanted to know more.

After having two fascinating conversations in the same week, I thought this book would be easy. I naively thought women were going to expose their female acquaintances and their friends' challenging behaviours. They'd spew it all out. I'd change the names and details. No one would know who was who. Like a free therapy session, they would express themselves and feel better for it.

Aren't women meant to be *the talkers*? I had visions of us getting right to the bones of the weird feminine behaviours over a bottle of wine. But it seems that women have also been taught the art of keeping their lips sealed.

I logged onto Facebook the following week and studied my friend list. I had more than 100 friends (perhaps after this book I will have a lot less), most of them female. I figured if most of these women can sit on Facebook for hours every week playing games, uploading image after image and commenting on someone's outstanding cake baking efforts or adorable baby, then surely they can find the time to fill out my questionnaire?

The questionnaire was about personal experiences with female friendships. The responses trickled in. In total, three or four women responded. I sighed, a lot. I guess women *are* busy.

That's when reality set in. This book wasn't going to be easy.

If I couldn't get my friends and acquaintances to reveal their negative friendship experiences in total confidence, then it seemed unlikely I would manage to get perfect strangers to be brutally honest.

Why was it proving so difficult to get the women in my life to open up and tell me what goes on with the females in their daily life or at least what had went on in their deep, dark past?

A few were polite and said they couldn't help as they had never experienced any negativity from women. I felt this was either a cop out, outright denial or blissful ignorance. Or maybe they were lucky sods. I thought how nice it must be to only experience coffee mornings, homemade jam and loving hugs.

Maybe I had just been incredibly unlucky or ridiculously misguided in my friend choices? I felt utterly stupid. It was maybe just me after all. I am simply a loser in this friendship game with a capital L stamped on my forehead.

But I couldn't accept this. I couldn't be the *only* woman out there with painful experiences.

Ignoring my ego, which was now a burst and saggy balloon, I patched it up with some sticky tape and carried on, regardless. I felt fatigued, burnt out, irritated and despondent by my relations with many women. I refused to accept my reality as folly. The hurt I had felt was real. It was piercing and stung.

The next type of response was, *"Yes, some women are bitchy, but I just stay away from them. I have no association with such women."* OK, better. There is something to work with here. At least some acknowledgement that women are prone to misbehaving with one another.

But the trouble with this response made me think that women believe they are simply able to stay away from troublesome friends. That it is easy to notice a negative friend and just step to the side. That they have a choice and can see a crazy bitch in their sights before she gets too close! Believe me, this is not the case. Often troublesome, negative women seek us out. They hide beneath smiles and loving hugs. And often their presence surprises us entirely.

Then there were a teensy-weensy amount of women who were frank and open. Interestingly, they were intelligent young women. They had experienced a lot of jealousy, bullying and unfair treatment from their female counterparts.

Relief swelled over me. (*It's not just me! I am not a complete loser in friendships – well, hopefully!*) My relief was coupled with grief for my friends who had experienced terrible pain at the hands of other women.

Then, of course, there was the non-response committee.

Perhaps they felt uncomfortable talking about personal feelings. For this very reason, I didn't push people. I assumed for some women it would be too painful and I respected that possibility.

I also concluded that for some women, the subject of my book was perplexing and they wanted no part in it. They did not want to support or encourage my 'woman hating' project (ridiculously unfair – I am in no way a woman hater. I'm only trying to *understand* women and how they behave.).

Or perhaps (I hope this was *more* likely) they felt they couldn't contribute in a meaningful way and so they said nothing. They didn't want to waste my time. They didn't have enough dirt. They had been luckier than me.

After many more months of silence drifting by, I decided I was pretty much on my own. I would have to wring out the few responses I received and lean on my family for support. Mostly, I would have to rely on my own reflections and personal experiences to write this book. Well, it turns out, lucky for you, I have a ridiculous amount of bad experiences to draw from. But despite having so much personal insight, I knew this would be one of the biggest creative challenges of my life.

For starters, it was never going to be an easy subject for a woman to discuss. It naturally makes females uncomfortable and close down ranks. The lack of responses confirmed this natural reaction. *Let's close the blinds and pretend no one is home, hopefully she'll bugger off soon enough. She thinks too much, she's too deep, too emotional. Leave me alone, you freak! Women are always lovely to me, you're the problem!*

Another issue with this book's subject is that I am going against the widely held belief that women are *always* nurturing and supportive to each other. Women are the carers. We look after each other and most days hold up the sky. We care for our families, soothe our babies, kiss away the tears. We are in many respects outstanding individuals.

However, females, by their very anatomy, nature and character, are complicated creatures.

Their behaviour sometimes contradicts the common rosy stereotype of feminism's idealistic 'sisterhood'. Sometimes a woman's behaviour towards another woman is *more* inhumane than accepting, engaging or fair.

What was really going against me was this notion of sisterhood. The sisterhood myth ensures women keep their lips sealed. To be disloyal to our own team is unacceptable or frightening. After all, we women have experienced years of oppression (mostly at the hands of men); we must continue to stick together.

Understandably, there is the belief that talking out negatively about females is surely wrong. We must boost each other, support each other and minimise the negatives.

Of course, I agree; we should encourage feminine solidarity. It is a beautiful and rewarding experience. It is essential for our social progress that women appreciate and consider other women. We should advocate loyalty and respect other women's differences. We cannot possibly create positive change in this world for women if we attack each other.

But equally, we must also accept that sometimes women do not stick together. Sometimes women rip each other to shreds in a frenzied verbal attack. Sometimes respect, solidarity and loyalties to one another are far from a woman's agenda.

With all these conflicting thoughts swirling in my mind, it was clear this book would be a tremendous challenge to complete.

For weeks, I thought I won't bother. Perhaps it is just too dangerous and I don't want to make waves. I don't want to provoke women and I don't want to plague women with dark thoughts about their own kind. What good could come from this book?

My conscious kept hissing at me. *This is stupid. Women will just hate you! They won't want to admit to this behaviour.* I stuffed a sock in her mouth. I was tired of smiling and pretending everything was okay.

I said to my over-active conscious - *I'd rather tell the truth, expose my female reality, than spend my life pretending that all is rosy in the garden with females, because you know and I know this – some gardens have more thorns than flowers.* She pouted and huffed.

I found that when I started writing this book, the words poured out. It was uncontrollable. I wanted to stop, but I couldn't. Did the truth of women like me need to come out? I'd like to think so. Was it now time to arouse debate and stimulate our awareness of what can go on between females? I thought yes, it probably is time to awaken and challenge our perceptions of women.

And so, despite all my doubts and fears, I carried on writing.

My name is Alana and I'm Not Perfect

I've always been the outsider. As a young woman, I tried countless times to 'get along' with females, but often I failed miserably.

Like many young women, I was emotional and sensitive, but I was to a large extent thoroughly logical. I couldn't quite grasp how females conducted their friendships. It always seemed incredibly complicated, fragile and fickle. And so it will be no surprise to hear that I enjoyed the company of males and found comfort in their good natured and often silly banter. It was a stark and inviting contrast to the seriousness of many young women. I had a lot of friends who were boys; it was *easier*.

It is also worth mentioning that I am a non-conformist. I'm hopelessly torn between being the shy girl who hides deep inside my being and the woman I am today who has strong morals, rock steady principles and a bucket load of opinions. I want to fight against the status quo and question everything. I want people to play fair. The truth is important to me, but I'm still finding my own voice. It's not an easy route, this desire to fight injustice.

I've always wondered why I have had such difficulties with females. Is it me? Am I the problem?

To a large extent, yes I am, of course, the problem!

I lack the ability to:

•Express myself neutrally

•Keep a low profile

•Agree whole heartily with a woman

•Fit in

•Flatter and appease females

•Ignore my principles

•Play by the strict social rules.

If you have a vagina – these qualities are a problem!

My tolerant, liberal spirit ensured I stood out. My inability to accept or ignore unethical behaviour possibly didn't help me either. My desire to revoke and rebel against shallow interactions was probably also a mark against me. I'd rather be alone than spend an hour listening to a group of women harp on about their house renovations. But most of all, I wasn't afraid to say the word **'no'** to females. This often resulted in explosive arguments and girls screaming down the telephone at me because I refused to back down to their little girl tantrums.

I stubbornly refused to forget my morals, my principles and my values all for the sake of being accepted into a cosy little clique. I'd rather be left out in the cold.

The result? I was mostly left out in the cold. My nose squashed up against the glass. Peeking in and wondering what I had said or done *this* time to warrant my rapid ejection?

Most of the time, I wasn't nodding and agreeing enough. I wasn't willing to roll out the red carpet to please a woman. I had failed to reply to yet another ten page email. I had not taken enough interest in *their* world (note: women *need* to feel important). I had disagreed with their idea or plans. I had the nerve to actually speak the fatal words, *"No, I'm sorry, but I can't help you,"* or *"No, I don't want to do that."* I had put my own sanity above and beyond their desires. I wasn't willing to flatter and please them just to be accepted. I had been my own person.

I've had brief episodes of being on the 'inside' of the female clique. It never lasted long; I was often rejected for my behaviour disturbing the group's fragile, but strict, status quo.

Often I even self-sabotaged my cosy position; perhaps deep down I knew I could never play 'the part' for a sustained time anyway. It pained me to just 'blend in 'or 'be a good girl'. I could never be moderate, agreeable and conservative for long enough. I knew I'd never be able to maintain a facade of being comfortable being a fourth, a third or even half of who I truly am, all in the interest of keeping the clique ticking along smoothly.

Furthermore, I've always been confused and disturbed by the way females can behave towards each other. I've been hurt and taunted, analysed and criticised, ostracised and rejected, prodded and judged many times by many girls and women. I've also witnessed women in my life experience great hurt and rejection from women.

It is with my deeply personal experience of females that I write this book. I want to share with you my own insights that highlight the worst of female behaviour and, more importantly, why I believe women may behave in negative ways towards you and me.

This book is not from a scientist who has studied the recent scientific results relating to female relationships or a psychologist who has interviewed her 200 clients. In fact, you could quite rightly argue that technically, I have no right whatsoever to write a book like this. I am not a therapist with a diary jam packed with public talks. I don't hold multiple top notch degrees in behavioural science. If anything, I am an ordinary woman who happens to know how it feels to be in the thick of things, who happens to know how it feels to be hurt time and time again by women. Don't see me as an 'expert'; see me as the 'friend' who you turn to whenever you encounter hurt. I've been there; I've felt what you feel.

After each wound and bruise, I cried or I was outraged. But most of all, I reflected. I desperately tried to understand what was going on around me with the women in my life and why they were behaving in very distinct and predictable ways.

It was a challenge to disclose these hidden truths to you in a way that is fair. No woman is perfect or without some negative traits and, of course, there are many women who conduct positive and healthy relations with each other.

This book focuses on the women who do not conduct healthy relations with women. There are some women who do not play fairly with each other. As you will see, some women display uncompromising, controlling and negative behaviour towards other women.

It is painful to acknowledge that sometimes women are not nice to each other. In fact, sometimes women actively want to hurt their female counterparts.

What is most shocking is that these women have a variety of different emotional tools at their disposal to cause hurt. These women have an array of passive aggressive behaviours ready to be implemented on other women when they see fit.

This book is not generalising that all women conduct their friendships in this negative manner; clearly and thankfully, this is not the case. However, there are enough women behaving badly to warrant a book.

***

This book is different.

There have been a lot of books written about the aggression and meanness that young girls and teenage girls subject each other to. As a society, we are all too aware of school girls and their inherent wickedness towards each other. It's socially acknowledged that school girls will play cruel emotional games on each other.

For many wounded grown women, the *'sugar and spice and all things nice'* rhyme is perhaps rather laughable. There is certainly a lot more spice and just a pinch of sugar in some girls!

I was blessed with three beautiful sons. If in the future I am blessed with a daughter, there will always be a part of me that will worry about how she will survive the physiological warfare that her feminine peers will bestow upon her.

Boys do not enjoy a childhood unscathed either. But it is the deeply personal and indirect aggression that tears at a young girl's very self–esteem. Her sense of self can be torn to shreds thanks to the employment of indirect aggressive behaviours.

With these thoughts in mind about young girls and teenage girls, we could quite rightly think that it is just 'girlhood' nonsense. A rite of passage that all girls will go through before they enter womanhood and mature.

Surely, most women learn to respect each other and grow up? Women are harmless and only want to nurture each other, right?

Sadly, as we will see, these school girl games do not magically end once we leave school behind. These cruel and manipulative behaviours continue to be played out between grown women.

This book is about the women who, despite being 35 years old, *still* behave like the cruel or manipulative school girls of our past. You may have grown up, but they have not.

***

This book is risky, but I must be brave (the truth is always risky!).

By publishing this book, I risk backlash and abhorrence from women. I risk being labelled a misogynist. A bitter woman with no friends. A betrayer of my own team. None of these labels are fair. As mentioned before, *trying to understand* female behaviours is quite different.

There have been chapters in my life, with regards to women, that were very bleak and depressing indeed. I have suffered great lows and bumps at the hands of women.

Wouldn't it be a cruel world if it is *women* who wish to silence me and beat me into submission? What irony after all we have been through to be heard and have a voice in society.

We must ask ourselves, why is it that women demand a voice, a platform for all matters that we are passionate about, but we are discouraged to express the *fears* we have about each other?

A frosty reception from women? Well, dear reader, it is a risk I am willing to take.

I've struggled with this book, but I am now determined to take you on this journey. I've nearly stopped many times. But I cannot allow my fear of female hostility to silence me. I wish to break the silence.

I have experienced great animosity from the most unlikely women and now it is time to fearlessly acknowledge that women are human and do hurt each other. We are not perfect. We are human beings.

***

A little clarity before we jump in.

Before we go any further, I want to clarify what this book is about. But first, let me tell you what it is ***not*** about. This book is not a witch hunt. I do not have an axe to grind with past demons or 'mean girl' bullies.

This book is not designed to incite negativity towards women in our society. It is not a reign of terror written to crush women and their hope for happy female friendships.

I am aware of how special and unique women's friendships can be when they are good and healthy. I am not here to tell you about the positive things as I am sure you can jump to the defence of women and tell me about the loyalty, the support, the unity you feel with your best girlfriends.

I ask you not to feel defensive - but to become reflective. I want you to consider my experiences and your own experiences fully.

What this book is about is truth. It is about reality. It is about the hidden world of female friendships that many men do not notice and many women deny exists.

It's easy to get the jitters and proclaim that most women are nice and what is the point in making such a fuss! But let's take a moment to understand that nothing in this book is far-fetched. It has happened to me. I'm not making a fuss. I'm telling you what goes on.

The truth is frank and sometimes painful, but we must accept our female reality. The only way to ensure we have healthy relations with women is to ensure we have healthy relations with healthy women. It's that simple. Furthermore, we also need to ensure we also behave in healthy ways.

This book will help you reflect on who your friends are, how they behave towards you and how you behave towards them.

This book is your insurance to a healthy future with females. Heed the warning signs; discover the truths and you should have the ability to allow only healthy female friendships into your precious world.

The harsh reality is this – women can sometimes behave badly towards each other. Let's get started. And stop kidding ourselves.

Jealousy

Want a woman to like you? Put a paper bag over your head and put on 50 lbs.

I'm going straight for the jugular first. It would be easier to start on a less hostile subject, but jealousy was a very common and prominent theme in my female relationships.

If you can understand jealousy in women and what causes their behaviour, you will be able to interpret a lot of what goes on around you with the women in your life. Things will become much clearer straight away.

What exactly do I mean when I say jealousy? Simply put, I am referring to behaviours that are begrudging and resentful. Jealousy can also include rivalry and power struggles between women. It can refer to passive aggressive behaviours.

But most of all, jealousy means the on-going dissatisfaction with one's own life and the inability to share in another person's joy.

Jealousy is at the core of many problems women face with each other.

Jealousy in any relationship is a mental cancer. It spreads to others and destroys all it touches. Every time jealousy touches your life, another part of your body and mind is wounded.

So where does jealousy stem from? It's not clear-cut. I wish it was simple. Given the inherent intricacies of relationships, a simple theory that captures the complexity of jealousy is probably unlikely. However, for your sake, I will certainly try to give you a theory to relate to.

Simply put, most jealous behaviour stems from insecurity and/or a deep unhappiness and/or dissatisfaction within that person.

Beneath their shiny façade and cheery smile, there is a dormant beast that can be disturbed at any moment. Are you provocative to the jealous person's emotional triggers?

You'll set off her jealous alarm bells and she'll instantly find it hard to love you if you are:

•A beautiful 19-year-old with legs up to your armpits.

•The new girl at work; you're friendly and everyone loves you. She's slipping further back from her boss's view and fears losing out on yet another promotion.

•You decide to have a baby and hey presto, you get pregnant instantly while she's been trying for ages.

•You find a new friend and get on brilliantly together. She feels pushed out and fears she is no longer important to you.

•You have no grey hairs, no wrinkles and no post-baby fat after three kids. She thinks you must be super human or some alien species.

If you are human and have been living on this planet, you will have experienced *some* form of jealousy. We have all been at the receiving end of jealousy and no doubt, we have all had our moments of crippling self-doubt and jealousy when we have compared ourselves to a friend or someone we admire.

It's a natural human infliction and women are, of course, humans. We feel all the same horrible, crippling, outrageous emotions that men feel.

We are women; we are not perfect, delicate creatures who are immune to outbursts and we are certainly not immune to other women projecting their jealousy towards us. Sadly, we do not have a protective suit to zip on whenever a jealous person decides they can't stand the sight of us!

Why are some women consumed by their jealousy?

Well, that's a tough question to answer. But I'll try.

I believe jealousy is more pronounced in cultures that attach social importance to marriage, material wealth and also in cultures that place a premium on personal property.

Some women will take these social pressures on-board and manage to cope well. They will not be susceptible to the jealous emotion despite the social pressures they feel. However, at the other end of the scale, you'll find women who are prone to jealousy and it will consume their daily thoughts.

These women who are more prone to jealousy may be more sensitive to social factors which are out of their complete control. Social factors such as: the importance within their culture of having a beautiful home, a challenging career, a romantic husband, perfect figure, cool friends, fabulous clothes, a shiny new car *and* a beautiful baby. Some women want *all* of these social ideals and they want it now! If those skinny bitches in Accounts can have it all, then why can't they? In cultures where just surviving the day is an achievement, women don't have the *luxury to desire* or compare themselves to friends; all focus is on staying healthy and alive. They have no time, money or energy to waste on creating the *perfect image*.

Jealousy could also come from one's own individual character and not from external or social pressures. Her individual character lives in a distorted reality. Her perceived reality and how she sees herself is blurred and distorted. She pokes and prods her relationships to death for answers. Certainty is a requirement at all costs, but it is unrealistic in this world. She is deeply insecure and nothing can satisfy her hunger. She will always compare herself and feel inferior to other women. Her self-esteem is low and her mental health is poor. Her jealousy is deeply ingrained within her, it speaks to her constantly, and she struggles to hear the voice of reason. This is possibly the most dangerous cause of jealousy as she is unable to step out; she is unable to stop her terrible thoughts. The jealousy is a parasite that lives inside her.

Another reason for a woman's jealous feelings could be a lack of parental attachment. It has been said by psychologists that if a woman did not attach with their mother and form a strong bond, she may be *more* vulnerable to negative emotions such as jealousy due to her **significant emotional loss**.

And lastly, she may be more prone to jealousy because she has a strong desire to be in *control*. She may be overly concerned about who is in the strongest position in any relationship she has. She may be constantly comparing herself, considering where she ranks in the hierarchy and ensuring she is top dog.

But what is the difference between male and female jealousy?

Women express it differently due to our cultural training. We are told from the moment we come out of the birth canal and the doctor clocks we have a vagina that we must be 'nice' and 'gentle' and we must 'suppress' our anger. We are pushed into a pink world of fairy cakes, butterflies and dolls.

Make no mistake - this gender bias plays a role.

It is socially unacceptable for a young girl to express her anger in a direct way. It is not 'lady like' to rant and rave, punch or kick. It is not 'ladylike' to mess around and push the other girls who are pissing us off.

A little girl's natural human reactions to adversity, anger and disgust must be modified and moulded. Her rough edges smoothed away to play tea parties with the other girls.

Young girls learn quickly to express their anger indirectly. They still have anger (just as much anger as little boys!), but they must learn to express it differently. A girl's anger must be invisible.

Little girls are inherently smart, they learn very quickly – in order to be acceptable - they must push their negative emotions underground and learn to be more passive.

As a result of this gender conditioning, girls learn to conceal, manipulate and keep the peace a lot quicker than their male counterparts.

In stark contrast, boys are allowed to express their anger directly; sometimes they are actively encouraged to be direct!

"Boys will be boys," the parents laugh at a children's birthday party.

The parents excuse the aggressive behaviour because boys are meant to behave badly and be rougher. It is to be expected. It is (unbelievably) acceptable. A little boy is seen as a wimp, a softie, a girl (as if being a girl is a negative thing!) if he is not assertive.

But, really, what nonsense! Isn't that a cop out? Is it wise to use a child's sex as an excuse for aggressive and poor behaviour? It is ridiculous that we *still* allow these sexist stereotypes so effortlessly into our homes even today.

Mothers have conversed to me, *"He's a boy, you know how rough and tumble they are. My daughter's such a princess, so much easier. But my son, he just won't listen; he can't be moulded, so why try? He's a boy, it's to be expected I guess!"* Isn't that fascinating? But why is *any* of this expected? This belief that boys can be a bit rougher, a bit louder, and a bit more wayward, but girls simply must be better behaved and more agreeable. We are told that girls are easier to mould and handle. And we drink it all up. Even if our daughter has *more* fighting spirit than a delicate fairy.

There is often sympathy for mothers with naughty boys, but if your girl is naughty and throws a mean left punch or lashes out at the girls in nursery, people ask, *"Why have you allowed her to become so aggressive?"* Society believes it is surely easier to *control* a little girl. Society believes it is easier to *control* females. If your boys are well-behaved, society is impressed and wonders what your secret is. How has a woman managed to control males? What's her magic formula? There is no magic formula. Girls and boys are simply children. They are not a different species.

Society judges our children. It tells us day in day out that our boys are rough and tumble, that our girls are delicate flowers. The pressures to mould our children into what a boy should be or what a girl should be is huge. It can be hard to fight back and allow our kids to be kids – messy, noisy, human beings with beautifully unique characters. But we must try to.

When it comes to gender conditioning, girls don't get off lightly. Girls can be preened and dusted to within an inch of their life. Is it any wonder that little girls can grow up to become such critical, jealous and angry young women? Is it any surprise when their emotional freedom was stolen from them at birth?

By contrast, little boys are allowed the freedom to work through their inner anger. And thanks to that freedom to express, most boys grow into men (after many years of direct aggression with their peers after the pub!) who are able to express their anger in a civilised, restrained way and it is usually direct and quick. They don't typically allow anger to dwell and fester. Usually, if a man is displeased with you, you'll hear about it from him. But for many girls, their emotional training is the polar opposite.

The result?

A bubbling, frothing volcanic emotional lava that lies underneath her subconscious.

Every so often the lava erupts (often due to a jealous trigger) in an uncontrollable fashion. She has had little or no training in how to constructively allow the resentments and jealousies to flow out slowly and calmly so nobody gets hurt. Remember, she has been socially conditioned to smile sweetly and keep all her outrage and hurt deep inside. Her anger, jealousy and frustration have been subdued. If she opens that pressure valve, the tension that is released is enough to knock you over!

***

What is most alarming about some women is their ability to hide their stewing jealousy. As we have seen, this festering jealousy is honed and perfected in girlhood. She learns to subdue her inner rage. She learns to smile, even though inside she is upset. She looks serene to you or me, but inside, she is conflicted. Inside, she is plagued with dark emotions and frustrations and she doesn't know how to express them. She simply can't or won't express them.

This dangerous and far more common jealousy among women is **silent jealousy**. It is the indirect, passive response to perceived threats.

It can be explained in a simple formula.

Indifference, disinterest, apathy from a woman towards YOU = She feels jealousy towards YOU.

How can you tell if a woman feels this silent jealousy and frustration towards you?

•When you are starting a new course and your friend doesn't wish you good luck or ask you how it is going. She shrugs her shoulders or ignores your attempt to progress in life. She might even tell you about her own course or job, but she seems unresponsive to your pursuits.

•When you have a gorgeous new man and she never asks how this new relationship is going. She probably fears he will come between your friendship. Her jealousy could also prevent her from feeling positive about your newfound happiness.

•When you are painting a picture and your friend never asks how you are progressing or simply says, "Well done!" for giving it a go. Maybe she would never have the time or ability to do such a project. Maybe she can't relate to your aspirations. Or maybe her jealousy of your talent is smothering her ability to cheer you on in your creative goals.

•When you are at a party and your friends never speak directly to you. They only speak about themselves. They make you feel like you are invisible. You struggle to get a word in. They are not interested in what you have to say. Any jokes, questions or comments you say are met with the bare minimum in response. They compliment each other and boost each other but try to ignore your presence.

On the other hand, you could simply have a thoughtless friend. She could just be pretty careless and not someone who is particularly responsive to other people. She may lack people skills or the attentive friend gene.

Of course, she could actually dislike you and not be interested in you at all; she is just waiting for the perfect time to slip out of your life and dump you.

But chances are, if she does claim to be a friend, and you can't help but notice that she is always unresponsive and resistant to your own personal happiness, then you probably have a jealous friend.

Jealousy in women means she does not ask you about your life, it means she doesn't care about what matters to you, it means she doesn't compliment you, congratulate you or cheer you on. She appears too preoccupied in her own existence and doesn't care about your contentment.

Your happiness, your success, your contentment makes her feel anxious and insecure. You make her feel undervalued. You make her feel like she is second rate.

It's not your fault; you can't help how *she* feels. She must help herself, but she can only stop her jealousy, or control it, if she first acknowledges the emotion. She is likely to be too strung up to think clearly. She is too twisted in knots, thinking you are happy/secure/pretty/confident/successful, to ever acknowledge her dark feelings towards you.

Often we ask, *"But why is she jealous of me? Little me? I'm really nothing special!"*

Jealousy is not rational. It can be hard to pinpoint, but it is no doubt a combination of factors. To break jealousy down further and understand why a friend is actually jealous of you, take a look at this formula. (I apologise for the formulas, but they help me.)

Comparison + Competition + Fear = Jealousy towards YOU.

•When a woman feels like her ego or self-esteem is under threat, she will feel jealous.

•When a woman feels like a friendship is under threat, she will feel jealous.

•When a woman feels undervalued and invalidated, she will feel jealous.

•When a woman feels second rate in your company, she will feel jealous.

Her jealousy is a proactive reaction to a threat. The threat she feels may be real or imagined.

The trouble with this **silent jealousy** is it is very difficult to detect. She will try to hide it. But if you're clever, you will pick up on her indifference. Her coolness. You will pick up on her disregard to the things in your life that matter. All will become clear. It is vital to trust your instincts.

Here's a clever way of knowing for sure…

Ask your friend to do something for you. Explain that her help would mean a lot to you and it would make you very happy. Make it clear how important this is to you. Think of a task that will benefit you; it should **not** benefit her. If she remains unresponsive, be careful. You may very well have a lethargic or busy friend, but chances are you have a woman who doesn't hope to make your life any sweeter than she currently perceives it to be.

Perhaps she cannot, or will not, encourage you because she knows she risks losing you? Perhaps she doesn't feel you should be granted your wish because she stubbornly believes you don't deserve her help? Are you already 'in debt' to her emotionally? Perhaps she believes she cannot relate to, or meet, your request?

There could be a multitude of reasons why your friend refuses to help. However, jealousy is very often at the core. Laziness, leading a busy life or simply losing interest in you as a person could also be the reason.

It is perfectly sane to make allowances and give your friend the benefit of the doubt, but if time and time again, she is apathetic towards your requests and aloof towards your successes, you could have a jealous friend.

For your own sanity, it would be wise to distance yourself from a jealous friend. You'll never please her. You'll never manage to banish her jealousy. That is her responsibility. Her own emotional health is for her to acknowledge and deal with. She needs to accept her own jealousies and make amends or seek professional help.

You should never stand in the shadows to make another person feel better about who they are. Stand up; let the light hit your face and your friends should cheer you on.

Always remember – when it comes to jealousy, it is the silence and disinterest of your 'friend' that says it all. She won't be able to share in your joy.

The cold hard truth about jealousy in women is this:

- If you have a healthy, happy relationship with your partner

- If you have a fantastic figure

- If you are pretty

- If you have a nice home

- If you have a flash car

- If you have an interesting career

- If you have good friends

- If you have spare cash

- If you have spare time

- If you have opportunity

- If you have ambition

- If you have love

- If you have sex

- If you have contentment

- If you have a flat stomach

- If you have beautiful breasts

- If you have gorgeous hair

- If you have principles

- If you have integrity

- If you have fertility

- If you have admirers

- If you have a voice

- If you have support

- If you have options...

A woman will feel jealousy towards you. That is a certainty of this life.

Women will always compare, compete and feel anxious as they will compare themselves to you or me. Women, who are jealous people, will rightly or wrongly always feel discontentment and dissatisfied in their own life. Jealousy is a huge pot that stews on and on. She can always find more reasons to be jealous of you.

Women are blinded by their jealousy. She will ignore your tears, your sadness and your depression. All she can see is your perceived beauty, your amazing life and your cool clothes. A jealous woman thinks, *What have you got to be upset about? You've got everything! Pull yourself together!*

She may disguise it well and pretend to feel your pain (all the time feeling smug that it's your turn to feel like crap – just like her!) or pretend to delight in your good fortune. She may even manage to convince herself that her feelings are authentic and her jealousy is minimal or contained.

She may refuse to recognise her jealous feelings and be surprised when they bite her and you. She may refuse to acknowledge her deepest, darkest feelings and tell herself, and you, that she is a sincere and genuine friend.

She may indirectly try to sabotage you – the threat. Indirect aggression or passive aggression is a woman's speciality. Jealousy very often promotes and encourages indirect aggression amongst women.

A jealous woman is often someone who cannot bear to experience themselves as a lesser light.

In order to shine brightly, she must rid the stage of brighter lights. I devised a little formula to remind us of the factors which encourage jealousy in women. (Oh, no! Another formula!)

Originality, creativity, excellence, integrity, beauty = offends and threatens a jealous person.

In short, your excellence to them is a form of persecution. Just by being you – she feels inferior.

Your 'light' makes her feel tormented, victimised and that life is unjust!

Your skills, your talents, your beauty, your happiness, your drive, your ambitions and your life makes her feel persecuted. You make her feel that life is unfair!

When her jealousy gets serious, when she is no longer able to contain her inner rage, she may resort to some passive aggressive tactics.

To make her feel better and boost herself, a jealous women may opt for: slandering your name, demoralising your sense of self, belittling your beliefs, criticising your talents, rolling her eyes at your dreams, scrubbing you from her Christmas card list and event lists, blocking you or deleting you on her social media, mocking your ambitions, excluding you from your very own social circle.

Her jealousy contorts her thinking and it ensures she behaves in a way to make you feel as rotten as she feels inside!

Jealousy is at the core. It breaks the spirit of people it touches and shatters communities. Just one or two jealous people can destroy a peaceful community or group of friends. Jealousy undermines and destroys all relationships. It never enhances or promotes positive relations between people.

Whatever happens, ensure you are aware. If you are aware, you have the power to make positive changes to your own life. It is fruitless trying to pretend that all is rosy and your friend adores you. If you have a 'funny' feeling in your tummy that she does not have your best interests at heart, then you could be right. A woman's instinct is often correct.

If you have a jealous friend, that is the greatest oxymoron. For, she is not a friend and cannot behave like a friend when she is inflicted with jealousy towards you. No matter how much she smiles and cuddles you - deep inside she is furious with you.

It is perfectly sane to take some big steps backwards. It is wise to start over and find healthier friends who cherish you, cheer you on and actively want to enhance your life!

**

The Green-Eyed Monster Stories

Note: *While the majority of these stories are mine, a small handful are from other women who have asked to remain anonymous.*

I had a friend who, whenever we went out for lunch, would always fish for compliments on the way her hair looked or the outfit she was wearing. I'm not being big-headed here, but I look after my own appearance, too. I do tend to wash my hair and pick out something nice to wear. She never once acknowledged my new outfit, beautiful jewellery or new bag. She only wanted to focus on her own material attributes. It became a one way street; I would emotionally preen her and try to make her feel more beautiful and validated as a person. Her own jealousy of me would not allow her to look at me and admire anything positive about me. She just ignored anything good about me and focused on herself. It was her way of coping with her jealousy. KC, 27.

**

I had just had a baby. I was very ill post-baby and had older kids to care of as well. My new baby was ill. My husband was ill, too. Awesome! I needed help desperately. We had no family nearby to chip in. Well, how do I put it? One of my friends criticised me for hiring a cleaner. Initially, she had been supportive and helpful, but once I hired a cleaner, she disagreed with my personal choice.

Was she jealous that I had the option of hiring in help? Who knows, but she made me feel guilty on Facebook in front of all my friends for wasting money on 'non-essentials'. But it was *our money*. How was it her business what we decided to spend our money on? The reality was we needed the help badly. I had a multitude of serious health problems that required medications, endless blood tests and finally, surgery. To top it off, just to add some more fun to the mix, I had postnatal depression and couldn't cope with daily tasks. To be honest, just getting the baby and me washed and dressed was a massive achievement. The last thing I needed was her posts on a social media website telling me and my friends I was being frivolous with my husband's earnings and maybe I could just manage my time better. I couldn't stand her superiority. I couldn't stand her smugness - *"Just clean when the baby sleeps, that's what I do,"* she said.

She had it all under control and my life was a mess. There was nothing helpful or supportive about her comments. I sank into a deeper depression and she had no idea of the impact her thoughtless words had on me. I already felt overwhelmed without her criticising my personal life choices. I ended up blocking her from Facebook, just to cope and regain some kind of control. She was angry and deleted me instantly. No questions asked. She just deleted me. I told her I was sorry, but her comments really hurt. She denied any wrongdoing and told me I was too sensitive. She refused to accept that she had been insensitive. I was making a drama out of nothing.

She was angry as she had washed some of my dirty clothes. She was angry as she had had a tough time after her child was born and she just got on with it; she failed to note that her mum lived in her house for the first 12 weeks. She also listed all the misery she had endured post-birth - not to show me compassion - but to show me that my situation was nothing major.

Within a few weeks, she hosted a party for one of my friends and she made sure I knew I was not invited. Everybody but the postman was invited. I was the bitch for blocking her comments. I sank deeper and deeper. The more I was socially isolated, the deeper I continued to sink. It's taken a very long time to find a spade and dig myself out of the huge hole I've been hiding in. I lost most of my self-confidence and most of my friends.

I lost quite a bit of weight after having my last baby. I was feeling great. My other friends were supportive, but this one friend refused to acknowledge my weight loss. She looked at me, shrugged her shoulders and said, *"Yeah, but you still have more to lose."* She was not interested in my efforts. She was competing with me and always telling me about how much weight she had lost. She wanted the compliments from me, but she refused to give me any. EB, 36.

***

My work is very female dominated. I was having a rough time and when a colleague asked how I was, I'm embarrassed to say I burst into tears. She quickly hugged me and with my blotchy red eyes, it was pretty obvious I was feeling vulnerable. There were at least eight other women sitting close by, none of them asked what was going on. Perhaps if I had gained weight and my husband had cheated on me they would have all rounded up, wiped away my tears and called him a bastard. They would be telling me I am beautiful and deserve better. But the reality is I'm a perfect size 10. I'm young. I have a happy marriage. I have beautiful kids. I mean, what could possibly be wrong in my 'perfect' life? They didn't want to know. Maybe they never noticed or maybe they did. I'll never know the truth. I felt invisible. C, 34.

***

A boy fancied me in school. He asked me out on a date and I took him up on his offer. I didn't fancy him, but I thought I'd give him a chance and maybe I'd find out he's a nice guy. I decided not to date him again. After all, I was only 16. I had plenty of time to have boyfriends and he wasn't really my cup of tea.

The trouble was there was a girl in my year who fancied him. He didn't fancy her. He was a free agent. When she found out I had went on this one date with him, she and her friends tormented me and made my daily life at school a living hell. They wrote on the toilets, naming me a slag, a slut, a bitch, a tart. They shouted at me, sneered, spat and ridiculed me. They stood outside my classrooms swearing and glaring at me. They launched an active campaign to break my spirit and self-esteem, but most of all, they tried to destroy my reputation. I was a virgin, but their slander was changing people's perceptions without a doubt. I was made to feel like a leper.

No other girl wanted to be seen with me. I'd try to approach a group of girls and they'd huddle together, shunning me as if I was a dangerous beast. None of those girls dared to look me in the eyes. They all believed the propaganda. No one questioned it. No one stood up for me and told them to leave me alone. Not one person in my year wanted to know where all this targeted hate and persecution was coming from and why.

I'd spend my lunch breaks on my own, often by a railway bridge. I thought, *This could all end now, this hell could all end. I just need to jump off this bridge.* But I couldn't do it. I couldn't do it to the poor train driver, I couldn't do it to my family and I was too stubborn to allow these girls to take my life. They had my present. They had my present in their hands and they were crushing the very life out of me. But they wouldn't take my future. I wouldn't allow it.

I'd walk back to school just before the end of lunch bell rang out. My heart beating, my hands and legs shaking, trying to hide the fear, trying to hold it all together for one more day. When would it end? Would they ever become bored of these cruel games? Would they never tire of tormenting me? How can these girls enjoy threatening me quite so much?

As time went on, the bullying showed no sign of stopping; it had become their daily habit like a cup of coffee or a morning jog. I couldn't live in fear anymore. I didn't deserve to be treated like this. I walked straight to the school office and quietly asked to see the school headmaster. I politely asked the ladies at the school office if they could please help me. I told them I was desperate and I must talk with the principal. They must have seen the torment creeping out from my red eyes or they must have seen my hands tremble. They told me to come into their office and sit down. Their compassion caused me to cry a little, but I had to stay strong. I needed to be able to explain what was going on. Thankfully, the principal was a good man and could see what was going on. *"These girls,"* he said, *"have a terrible case of jealousy and it will stop. I promise you, Alana."* The bullying only stopped when he excluded the ring leader.

***

I started a new project at work. I was given a big leg up by my boss after years of hard work. It was a great promotion. I was very excited! At last some recognition for all my hard work. I noticed how most of the women who claimed to be a mate simply did not acknowledge my promotion or if they did, it was a very cool and quick, *"Well done."* They did not bask in my glory. They wanted my moment to be over quickly so the focus could return to them. It was a real eye opener. When I was the same as them – their equal – they 'loved' me. It was fun, but as soon as I tried to better myself and progress, they were pissed off and rejected my success. I was different. I wanted different things. Being a woman and being different or wanting to be recognised can be social suicide! J, 29.

***

Kat was jealous of the friends I had at school and so she decided one day to destroy my 'perfect' little world. I was 14. She was 16. I'd known her for some time and we had become close - the kind of fast, instant intimacy that teenage girls always have. She had already left school and was working. It was an odd friendship as I was only 14. But she always said how mature I was. I looked up to her and asked her for advice. I told her my secrets, she told me her secrets. I fancied this boy. A stupid school girl crush. I was not hopelessly in love. He was going out with my school mate. He treated her so nicely and I guess I longed for that, too. I didn't love him; I just wanted to feel loved and cared about. I desperately wanted to feel loved - I was a hopeless romantic, changing my mind like the weather. It's a difficult time - the hormones are racing, emotions are high.

I'd never have told my friend at school. It was pointless as I knew my feelings would soon pass. But Kat's jealousy changed everything.

She wanted to come out with me and some of my school friends to a disco. I must have hesitated for too long in my reply. I didn't jump and scream and do all the stupid things girls do to make each other feel wanted. She started screaming at me, *"You don't want me to come? You nasty little bitch, I'll show you. I'll show you! Just you wait!"*

Show me what? This didn't sound favourable. I tried to get her to calm down. I tried to reassure her that I loved her and wanted her in my life. But she caught a whiff of my uncertainty and she couldn't hear me anymore. The truth is - I'd been finding her intense and demanding. I was scared of her. She was impossible to say no to. She was moody and always pouted if I was not focused on her entirely.

She went straight to the boy's door. Knocking furiously, she blurted out that I loved him and would do *anything* to get him. He was shocked. His parents were shocked. I was mortified. I wanted to die. I didn't really know how to undo her lies. I didn't love him and I wasn't going to say or do *anything*.

It wasn't long before I become a threat to my school friends. I had broken the rule book by having this crush. It wasn't long before they ostracised me. No matter how many times I said I was sorry and cried - I was now untrustworthy. Kat had destroyed my reputation - fuelled by her jealousy. She left my life in tatters. I never saw her again. It horrified me how much power she had over me and how she abused that power. I was shocked at how jealousy can destroy all it touches.

***

Quotations on Jealousy

In jealousy there is more self-love than love.

Francois de la Rochefoucauld

Jealousy is a tiger that tears not only its prey but also its own raging heart.

Author unknown

The jealous are troublesome to others, but a torment to themselves.

William Penn

To cure jealousy is to see it for what it is, dissatisfaction with self.

Author unknown

Jealous people poison their own banquet and then eat it.

Author unknown

Intensity

There is something intense and disturbing about the way some women conduct friendships.

Women like to get under your skin. Women like to be central in your life and central in your thoughts. Women have a strong need to connect with each other.

The desire for a connection is a normal, healthy desire. We all hope to be understood, to be accepted, to be loved for who we are.

It is a beautiful experience when your friend loves you warts and all, come rain or shine. No matter what happens, she unconditionally loves you and accepts you. In her company, you feel reassured, relaxed and supported. They have our back and they really 'get' us. They understand us. They know us and we know them. It feels good to be appreciated and cherished.

However, in some instances, the intensity can be **suffocating**.

Sometimes women mistake intensity for close friendship, when, in fact, it is not a friendship; it is simply her control and her power over you that you are experiencing. If she loses her power over you, you will risk ejection from her life. There is nothing accepting or unconditional about this kind of intense friendship.

What's the problem with this intense friendship?

Her expectations of you are enormously high. She believes your friendship, your time, your love are her right, her entitlement. She has invested time in you; you must invest time in her or she will effortlessly detach from your life without so much of a flinch. All loving memories of your time together will be forgotten. You have not met her emotional needs; you're dumped, sister.

With intensity and closeness come **obligations and expectations**. For some women to feel secure and happy in their friendships, they need constant emotional preening and constant praise. They will demand your full attention. She must be number one in your mind. She doesn't care if you have just had a major operation or had a baby. She needs your attention and she needs it pronto!

They demand that you are part of all social events. It can become like a premier football team. If you slow down and can't keep up with the training schedule, then you won't make the team. You're a slacker. For God's sake - just work through your injury!

They decide that you just don't care *enough*. You don't pull your weight and make the effort. They can always find another woman who is willing to meet their desires, needs or demands. They can always find another vulnerable soul who is blinded and seduced by their smile and charm. There is always another woman who is only too happy to please her.

The reality of female friendships is actually very simple – **women expect far too much from each other.**

Their expectations upon their female friends are enormous. You must be her confident, her everything, her life blood. You must be there for her and always be willing to help and support her.

A woman demands, expects or desires deep and meaningful emotional support from her female friendships.

Men don't expect much from their friendships at all.

The word to really focus on here is *expectation*.

Men have a much easier time.

They have very little expectations of each other.

A man will **not** *'be there'* for a close friend from one year to the next. He will become a father, he will go through a rocky patch with his health, and he will lose his job. His friend will call him out of the blue years down the line and they will joke and laugh as if they just spoke yesterday.

He does not need his friend to hold him up or support him. **He does not expect anything from his friend.** Perhaps it would be nice to have a supportive mate, but it's just not 'manly' to bitch and moan about a friend. And anyway, he is delighted to hear an old familiar voice *after* the bad times he has had.

He holds no grudge, no bitterness about what his friend has missed in *his life*. In the big picture – it is really no big deal. They're talking now and having a laugh!

Men might not be perfect at many things in life, but they certainly know how to keep their friendships intact and going long-term. In fact, they are masters at maintaining long-term friendships. They do not dissect their friendships, they do not over analyse. They do not expect much at all.

Isn't that refreshing? Perhaps women could learn something from the guys? Instead of women thinking they are experts in the friendship field, maybe – just maybe – the men have got the right approach?

Consider this.

When men make new friends and hang out with old friends, they rarely get *too* personal.

They have no desire to offload or express their deepest, darkest feelings. Men are masters at keeping a safe and respectful emotional distance from other men.

Another thing men tend to do is try to see the good in their friends. Friends who are arsehole drunks or raving lunatics are often forgiven time and time again, *"He's a good bloke, really. I've known him for years! Give him a break!"* They try not to judge and they try not to pry. They accept that they themselves are far from perfect. They understand that they also make mistakes. They will take the piss and highlight their friend's shortcomings.

This is an interesting approach. It's interesting to compare the male approach to the delicate, tentative and intimate manner that women display towards each other.

Men talk about *'safe'* subjects like sport, work, and comical stories about the past. They have no intention of rooting around, asking personal questions or finding out what makes their friend tick as a person. There is no hidden agenda. They have no need to make a deep and meaningful emotional connection with a friend.

That's worth repeating.

Men have little need to make a deep and meaningful emotional connection with a friend.

Women have a greater need to make a deep and meaningful emotional connection with a friend. And the quicker it happens, the better!

But whoa, slow down there, lady! What's the rush?

Maybe that's where women go horribly wrong.

Women seem preoccupied with getting to know female friends deeply, instead of simply enjoying their company.

Women seem determined that their friends must accept and understand them completely, even if they struggle to accept and understand *themselves* completely.

Women seem determined to get to the bones of the matter and truly know other females inside and out.

Women are either hot or cold. Women are hugely invested or they are detached. There is little room for middle ground. There is little room or time for the casual meaningless and good bantered chat that men specialise in.

With women, you are either in or out. You either adore her or don't care enough. She is either important to you or her very presence is not vital to your daily life. How do you feel about her? She needs an answer now!

The truth is most women invest a huge amount of time, sweat and tears into every new female friendship. It is no wonder we feel like we deserve their time, sweat and tears back.

It is little wonder women expect so much from each other as we invest far too much of our emotional energy. We are exhausted and we need our female friends to replenish us with 'emotional fuel' quickly.

But why? Why do we desire these incredibly close bonds with each other? Why do women feel the need to emotionally connect with perfect strangers – *"Oh, I know what you mean. The very same thing happened to me!"* What is driving this urgent behaviour, this intense desire to connect?

I have a few theories I'd like to share with you.

Women might require close bonds with one another in order to feel safer in this unruly and unpredictable world. The world can still be incredibly dangerous for women. We may be stronger than ever, but we are still vulnerable and it makes sense to band together in cliques or dyads.

Another theory has narcissism at the core. There is something narcissistic about women's friendships. For one, we are typically drawn to women who are like us in appearance, social status or education. Like the Greek youth, Narcissus, we fall in love and admire our own reflection.

Women are also incredibly interested in their own life and they crave to have a friend who is as equally interested in their life. Of course, to achieve this ideal, we must first show great interest and invest time in the potential friend. We must preen her and groom her emotionally.

In theory, we believe, she should return the social favour and show interest in us. Due to our deep need to be validated and appreciated, we forge close bonds very quickly. If she does not return the favour, if she does not emotionally groom us back and tell us how wonderful we are (...*and after all my time and effort – that ungrateful bitch!*), there could be trouble brewing.

Another narcissistic quality of female friendships is that some women believe the universe revolves around them. They are absorbed by their own life and will do anything in their power to gain your worship and appreciation of their grandiose illusion.

It is all too easy to jump on board and be consumed by these women. It looks dazzling to our ordinary life. We think we matter to them and that we are important people in their life.

But often we are left hurt when we realise they have little interest in who we truly are. They have no concern for our feelings or needs. Their own desire to lure you in, trap you and employ you as a devoted admirer is just too great for them to care about you!

My other theory of why women are prone to intense friendships is because they never had a secure attachment with their mother.

These women may spend their entire adulthoods trying to recoup the huge emotional loss of their mother's lack of love or approval. They may try to be the domineering mother figure to their friends or they may be the vulnerable child who desperately needs your attention, your approval and your validation. Perhaps a combination of the two characters will emerge depending on her emotional state that day.

It should be noted, I am not particularly attached to any of these theories. It is perhaps a combination of these factors that contribute to why a woman has a deep desire to have an intense relationship with her female peers.

Each and every woman will vary greatly in her intenseness and why she conducts her relationships in this way. It is almost impossible to be sure.

But I can be certain of one thing; women do behave in this way. It happens every day in schools, universities, work places and even between the wholesome looking mothers waiting for their kids to come out of class.

The question is – are *you* able to keep a safe and respectable distance?

***

Intensity Stories

I couldn't make my friend's event. Sadly, I had just miscarried my unborn baby. I was distraught, bleeding and in pain. I was 21 years old.

I never heard from her and then, weeks later, I received a letter. I picked up the light pink envelope from my doormat and recognised the writing instantly. Anxiously, I gently opened it, but her words tore at my heart. She condemned me for missing her party. She was furious with me for not thinking of her and considering her party important. She said she thought I was a close friend and close friends make the effort.

Our friendship never survived that letter. She could never forgive me for missing her party that meant a lot to her and I could never forgive her for her lack of compassion.

Our expectations of each other destroyed our friendship. It still makes me feel sad to this day.

If I had just took lots of pain relief, took a bag full of sanitary towels to ebb the heavy current of blood and put on a big smile that night – she would have been so pleased and we'd probably still be friends.

But I just couldn't face a party. I didn't have the emotional or physical strength. I was bent over in agony, my unborn child ejected from my womb. And now I had to face the pain of losing a friend.

It was such a waste of a friendship. I did try to reach out to her and move forward, but there had been too much disappointment. I was already in her debt emotionally, there was little chance she could summon up more empathy to support me anymore or feel compassion for my deep sorrow.

I discovered that women are humans; they need the love and attention back that they give out, even when we have no ability to do that at the time. I desperately wanted to love and support her back, but I was too broken by my loss.

**

I couldn't make my friend's kid's party. I had a very good reason, but she wouldn't listen. I can understand her feeling let down by me. We had never had any arguments or problems in years, but by me missing the party - our friendship died that very day. Her expectation was that I would be there no matter what. I was never invited to anymore of her parties. She found some new friends who she felt were more reliable, more committed to her life. I wish she could have listened to my reason! But now looking back, it was probably a blessing as it was only a matter of time before I fell short and I was kicked out of her life. K, 35.

**

I had this best friend at school. I saw her all day at school. It was the intense, close-knit bond that teenage girls excel in. If I didn't call her as soon as I got in the door after school, she would be moody with me. One day, she phoned me up an hour after school and was screaming down the phone at me because I had not phoned her quickly enough! The final straw was when she was arguing with me and telling me that I didn't care about her. She wanted me to surprise her and organise her birthday. I couldn't manage to organise it and she went mental. I screamed, *"I'm not your mother!"* Needless to say, the friendship ended.

**

We'd draw pictures of each other and write letters to each other daily. We'd see each other all day at school and hang out all weekend, just singing and dancing and talking for hours. In many ways, a girl's first love is her best friend and when that friendship ends, she is heartbroken. I invested every inch of myself and I know she felt as passionately about me.

***

If you want to know what heavy expectations can do to a relationship, take a few moments to consider this story.

I'd literally just stepped through the front door. I'd travelled all the way from Scotland with my three kids and we were exhausted, but finally, we were back in Australia. My head had barely touched the pillow when the telephone rang out. I knew already. My mum was calling to tell me that my grandmother had died. She had died within hours of us leaving Scotland. She had held on tightly, squeezing every last hour with me and her great-grandsons. But now she was dead. I sank into my bed. I knew she was dying, but I hadn't expected her death to happen so suddenly. My grandmother meant the world to me. I had travelled across the world to say good bye to her and kiss her one last time. She was not some distant relative, she was my gran, and I loved her with all my heart.

After sleeping for some hours and dreaming of my grandmother, I got up and checked my emails. There, in my inbox, sat an email from a close friend, one who had sadly been too busy to see me during my recent trip back to Scotland. She knew my gran had *just* died - her body *still* warm. But her email had no compassion or acknowledgement of my loss; she only apologised for not being able to see me. It was a short and snappy email, upbeat even. She wasted no time telling me about her impending wedding and the theme she was trying to create. I tried to take in her words, but they washed over me. She had emailed me for a favour. I was to call my mother and ask her to *source* a particular type of ribbon for my friend. I guess it must have been awfully important to her and she simply couldn't wait for my grief to process. My mother had previously made beautiful wedding cards; this friend had assumed my mother could source cheap ribbon due to having contacts in the wedding industry.

Do you know that feeling when you are numb inside? I guess that is how I felt. I was worried about my parents in Scotland. I was worried about how my dad was coping with his mother's death. I was worried about how my sons would handle the death. But this friend, she was furious and utterly disgusted with me when I said,

"No, I won't be asking my mum to source ribbon for you. She is rather busy with my dad right now."

I had said the word **No**. All hell broke loose. I had hoped she would see her insensitivity and perhaps apologise. I would have moved on because it is natural for brides to get a bit self-absorbed with their wedding plans. But I had said **No**. I had refused to meet her desires.

She deleted me from Facebook almost instantly. She then telephoned my sister-in-law to complain about how unreasonable I was. She was outraged that I was not willing to do her '*a little favour*'. She made many flawed stories up about my family and me, she distorted the truth and she clutched at straws to prove she was the victim. She wanted to believe that I was unreliable, that I was a hopeless friend to her. Thankfully, my sister-in-law is a woman who is best described as someone with an astute intellect, someone with a canny awareness and an even sharper wit. She was able to see through this woman's drama and understand that this was *not* the reaction of a friend.

No one has a perfect life. We all have stresses and strains in life. No doubt this friend was having a bad week, a bad year, perhaps, but we can't throw tantrums, we can't attack the very people who love us whenever we don't get what we want from them. It's not fair. It's unethical. To launch a verbal assault at an unsuspecting relative about a grieving friend seemed inhumane.

Meanwhile, I was huddled up in bed, unable to eat, unable to sleep. Losing a close friend, the same day I lost my grandmother, seemed like a mighty blow. Having a close friend *attack* my character seemed like a cruel dream.

I didn't meet her expectations. I was not willing to please her. I put my own sanity and my own family *before* her superficial desires. I will never apologise for putting my family first. I failed to meet her warped expectations. I've never heard from her since she deleted me and telephoned my sister-in-law. She exploded in rage, spat up grievances and spewed ridiculous lies. It was deplorable how she behaved during a vulnerable chapter in my life.

***

Quotations on Intensity

Happiness is not a matter of intensity but of balance, order, rhythm and harmony.

Thomas Merton

I do not think that obsession is funny or that not being able to stops one's intensity is funny.

Jim Dine

The best lack all conviction, while the worst are full of passionate intensity.

William Butler Yeats

The curse of the romantic is a greed for dreams, an intensity of expectation that, in the end, diminishes the reality.

Marya Mannes

Power Games

For some women, being part of a group or a dyad is not enough - she must be queen bee. She must be central to the friendship and she will stop at nothing to ensure she is in control and has the power. She must be the one pulling the strings.

If she considers you a threat, she will want to get rid of you or keep you down. She has many tactics to snub you. She has many tactics to keep you from stealing her thunder.

Her own personal demons drive her to replace you or, at the very least, transform the dynamics of the group. She needs to leave a legacy, even if it is a negative one.

You may think your acceptance and compassion is enough. You may tell yourself that love can conquer all her insecurities, but your love and acceptance is not enough. She can't help play these cruel games. It is who she is.

All it takes is one woman to destroy your relationships with a group of women. Just *one* woman.

The question is – will you allow it? Will you even notice the games?

Most women do not notice until it is too late.

If you have ever been unlucky enough to encounter an alpha female figure in your life, you will shudder to think what games she is currently playing on the 'friends' she currently has.

If you were lucky, you got away unscathed, perhaps a little dizzy and confused. If you were unlucky, she may have turned your life upside down to ensure her life was how it needed to be. You're quite possibly still licking your emotional wounds from the fall out.

In an all-female group, a woman might strive to become the female equivalent of a primate alpha male. She must conquer. She must win. It pays to watch an alpha female in action – from a safe distance!

Beneath her sweet smile, she is fierce, cunning and motivated. She has an agenda and she will meet it at all costs. She knows what she wants and she knows how to achieve her goals.

What is her goal? What is her hidden agenda?

Her goal is usually adoration, acceptance and validation from the other women. This all sounds harmless enough. But, of course, in her pursuit to the top spot, there will always be other women who will be pushed out of her way.

The ambitious newcomer who plays this game has two choices in order to accomplish her goal. She will either become intimate with who she perceives to be the important women or she may bond with the weaker members. The women *she* perceives to be weak. In her mind they are easy targets. She may use these weak members' vulnerability to her advantage and gently manipulate their insecurity. Her weak targets can be enrolled at a later date for a future takeover bid.

The weak members will feel appreciated and wanted – a long awaited ego massage. They are no longer invisible or unimportant. The alpha female can latch on and benefit greatly from these vulnerable souls who, of course, also just want to be loved and accepted.

How do these power-crazed women achieve these cruel goals of take over?

Watch and learn. She is a master of deception. Manipulation is her middle name.

Her clever tactic is this – First, she will become utterly indispensable to you. Nothing will be too much trouble. You will think, *I don't know how I ever managed to live this life without her in it!*

She will mother you. She will emotionally groom you – primate style.

She will lure you in with juicy gossip, flattery, a fantastic lifestyle that is open to you, a willingness to be helpful.

Catering to your every whim, every errand, every problem, and every worry. How can you resist such a wonderful and agreeable person?

Many of us are so utterly starved of this affection that very few women will allow the attention to concern us.

It just feels so good and she is just so nice, funny and helpful! It would seem too negative to suspect any agenda from a new friend.

The result - you will be besotted by her.

You will be amazed by her generosity. You will feel soothed and loved. You will stand up for her and insist she is a good friend and she loves you unconditionally. You will minimise any traits that seem dubious. She has a kind heart and she only wants to help, that's what friends do – they help each other out. Anybody who tells you she has hurt other people *must* be wrong as she is so nice to you!

Once a woman is considered as indispensable to a group – her soiled information, her gossip, her lies and her words will become Dogma.

She is *now* dangerous. And often we haven't a clue!

Next, she will take up much of your social life. She will literally take over! You will see her wherever you go, so you will always have her name close to your thoughts. She will take you to events or arrange her own events to enhance your life. You will enjoy new experiences. She feels like the sister you never had.

Then, she will convince you that you *only* need her. How does she achieve this?

First, she will manage to socially isolate you. Then, when she has your full attention and your loyalty, she can slander and gossip about your previous friends.

Her smear campaign will only show your friends in a negative light. There will be nothing fair or objective about her opinions. This is done slowly and tactically to not arouse suspicion of her agenda.

She will ensure she looks like an exceptional friend or a victim; the others are average or deceitful and can be forgotten about.

Life can only be glorious, safe and certain with her in your life. She is the loyal and reliable one. Forget about the rest!

She is now in a very strong position. You are now in her emotional debt. You have received a huge amount of time, investment, information and emotional grooming from her so, of course, you feel loved and validated. You feel important. Very often you will repay her with love and validation.

How does she achieve this goal of power so easily?

It's simple; no woman wants to believe she has been fooled by a manipulative woman playing a game. Everyone's ego wants to believe our friend adores us because we are wonderful and interesting people.

She picked me because I am a great person!

Everyone wants to believe we are clever enough to pinpoint negative behaviour. We think we are supremely clever and a woman will never fool us.

She'll never pull the wool over my eyes! I heard she was a bitch to her other friends, but there's two sides to every story. Maybe they were horrible to her! And anyway, she's always nice to me! You naturally comfort yourself with this belief.

We tell ourselves, *We'll be aware and tell her straight if she does try any funny business!*

But often we don't realise this until it's too late. Often we don't notice until we are in too deep. We can't believe we were so blind. We can't believe we never saw who she was. We can't believe we ignored the warnings or that we didn't listen to our instincts.

The women who conduct these power games so effortlessly pick you from a group because you are the easiest target. If there is a weak link in a group of women, she will target the link that sags.

Some power queens do go for the most important women. Some just can't resist the challenge.

These power-crazed women know they can simply deny all wrong-doing. They know some of her 'friends' will believe her innocence. She knows some of her 'friends' will be blinded by her and accept her words as the truth, as dogma.

But typically, it is safer for the alpha female to remain unexposed and target the less socially strong women.

Whatever her strategy for take-over – it is usual for her to try and remain undercover. She does this by only seeking out specific characteristics - unquestioning, accepting women are favoured. Someone who is unlikely to blow her cover. They may be important forces to a group or weaker members – but they must appear emotionally vulnerable and ripe for picking. Some women are easy pickings. Some women give off an aura of neediness which is perfect for take over.

When you have an alpha female in your midst, and you become conscious to her games, you are now in dangerous waters. You have introduced her to your friends. She made herself helpful to them and not before long, she will begin to gossip about you, telling them little half-truths and lies about you. She will create bad will about you amongst your friends. It will become too exhausting to undo all her gossip. Your former friends will lose all respect for you and you will naturally lose respect for them.

How can I have friends who are so easily fooled? you'll ask yourself in despair. You thought your mates knew you! But they have been duped, sucked in and sucked dry by an alpha female and all because you introduced her, accepted her and welcomed her into your little social circle. Whoops!

What will astound you is that no one in your group of friends will find anything remotely suspicious about a newcomer who flatters and emotionally grooms with such ease. Her sleekness blinds. Her cunning and rampant exuberance for our life impresses.

Time and time again in groups of women, most members will feel little suspicion and even more shocking - most will not bother to alert the friend who is gossiped about.

Why does this happen so easily? How can you have friendships one month and the next month – the women are perfect strangers to you?

Basically, women in groups find it almost impossible to carefully interrogate and question the alpha female who spreads idle gossip.

It is also hard for some women to resist the temptation of spreading the gossip.

Women have learned to look the other way. When an alpha female behaves in a manner that is unethical or unfair towards another woman, it is much safer to just look the other way, as opposed to directly question the behaviour or gossip.

After all, it is not happening to *them*. They are okay. They have not seen anything happen.

Then there are the women will also habitually join in and delight in the juicy gossip. They will be intrigued, mock shocked and have their own opinion on the gossiped about. They will become agreeable. They will show compassion towards the person who is gossiping. They will listen intently to the person who is gossiping. They will nod, sigh, gasp and encourage the gossiping woman to say more.

It is vital to understand why groups of women allow this to go on.

The main culprit is this – **women are emotionally needy. They are emotionally greedy**.

Therefore, women are reluctant to stop an alpha female or a group of women from excluding or scapegoating or gossiping about an individual woman because they are scared the group could turn on them next.

It is safer to be agreeable to the slander or to look the other way. It is rarely safe to question the slanderer.

Most women are reluctant and understandably afraid to stand up to a group of women, or even one alpha female, who is in their midst.

If they stand up for themselves or for the woman being emotionally torn to pieces, she is highly likely to be tossed to the side and rejected, too. It is far safer to join in or simply listen. She can remain securely nestled in the group.

Therefore, it can be said that women habitually sacrifice their honesty, morals and principles. They overlook or make excuses for poor behaviour. They are able to overlook the ostracism of their peers. They are willing to join in with the bitching and sabotage of other women. All to ensure they themselves are not rejected from the group.

Simply put, a woman's natural yearning for love and attention, for approval, acceptance and understanding from another woman can leave us vulnerable to alpha females posing as maternal and nurturing figures.

Our desire for the love of a female friend can leave us wide open to feminine con artists. Our neediness can leave us at risk and little Miss Power Games uses our neediness to her full advantage.

***

I wish this was the end of the chapter. But there are more power games. Hang tight, reader. These games are worth knowing about.

Women can be quick to judge. Quicker than the speed of light, in some cases. Women judge themselves quickly and often harshly, make no mistake – they judge women and measure other women by their own harsh yard stick.

But we want to see the best in other women. We want to show them compassion and we believe they want to show us compassion.

You have a friend and she behaves in a way that disturbs you or upsets you. You want to forgive her and be compassionate, so you let it go. You decide to give her the benefit of the doubt. You tell yourself,

She didn't really mean to do that or say that to me, just let it go!

But she did say it or she did do it. There's a strong chance it could happen again. But you ignore your conscious. You don't want to make a scene and sound overly sensitive. You don't want to lose her. You know speaking your mind and confronting her could mean the friendship is over. Female friends rarely last after a confrontation.

Then, out of the blue, you trip up and make a mistake that in some way upsets her.

She has never once acknowledged any of her past behaviour. She thinks she has a perfect friend record and now feels entitled to condemn you.

Her softness turns to hardness overnight. She wasn't perfect and you knew this, but this is just ridiculous. Her coldness towards you shocks you to the core.

What happened to her compassion? Why can't she find forgiveness like you did? Has she lost her mind completely?

She can't and won't forgive you. She is playing a power game with you. It was only a matter of time before she climbed up on the roof and took the moral high ground. It is just too tempting for these women!

At last, you – yes, you - little Miss Perfect – she has some dirt on you and she will enjoy every moment of you squirming and begging!

***

I couldn't write a chapter on power games without including the power games that are effortlessly illustrated between teenage girls every day in schools all over the world. And some grown women still can't help themselves. Old behavioural habits that were executed daily in the school yard take a long time to change.

So what are the rules of this game?

Just one misguided comment, one silly step, one stupid mistake or one wrong look and you risk being rejected.

You also risk rejection if you are not supportive enough, if you are not pretty or cool enough, if you are not agreeable enough, if you are not attentive enough, if you are too different from the other females, or if you are someone who misses important events in their life. You're booted out of camp, sister!

It is understandable why women are a little nervous around each other.

Study a group of women. Watch closely how they monitor and self-regulate what they say to each other. Most will be very wary of how they come across to the other women. Most women will refrain from telling a woman what she really thinks. Most women do not want to risk causing offence. Most will self-censor their own words and actions.

Authentic or independent thought can lead to ostracism or criticism. Rather than risk social rejection, women will use indirect and passive aggressive behaviours. Some women will seem on edge, others will manage to hide their anxiety. But most women, deep down inside at some point, will say to themselves, *"I hope she didn't take offence at that comment today,"* or *"I hope she will invite me to the next event."*

Ask most women and they will agree they do feel their words and actions are most harshly judged by other women. Not by men, but other women. We are our own harshest critics and we understand that other women are equally harsh on us.

Therefore, it is hardly surprising that women and girls all over the world are presently being rejected and ignored by females who they thought only yesterday was a close friend. But we just spent a weekend away together, danced till 4am and shared all our deepest secrets! Hang tight, honey. These things happen.

It is imperative to explain this clearly. For a woman to be rejected by another woman – it is quite possibly the most gruelling and painful emotional experience. She will be wounded for life. To be rejected by her own kind will turn her blood cold. She will feel like an emotional leper.

Every woman knows the pain of female rejection. To our ancestors, it meant certain death. To today's modern woman, it means social suicide. She will need to try her hardest to be welcomed back or leave with her head down. Her dignity and self-respect destroyed by another woman's condemnation.

In woman world, if you happen to be truthful and speak up about your rejection, your ostracism at the hands of females - you endanger the status quo. You are likely to offend other women. The harsh truth startles. Many women will avoid you. It is almost impossible to protect your name once it has been slandered and gossiped about. It is almost impossible to be heard. You lose your power, you lose your voice.

Despite the difficulties involved, it is imperative that women stand up for themselves and for other women who are being victimised by power games. It is vital that women remain true to their good moral code and disconnect from women who bully and manipulate, even if that means social suicide.

These power games can happen to anyone and it does. Often the most unlikely women are ostracised and condemned. Often the most unlikely women are the bullies.

It is about power. It is about safety in numbers. No one is willing to speak up for the rejected woman. They, of course, fear they could be next.

They may also feel the rejected woman is a dubious person anyway and she deserves her fate. She had it coming! There is no room for compassion; there is no room for understanding. There is little room for reasoning or fairness. Judgements have been made.

No one asks why have we actually bothered to reject this woman? Isn't this punishment a bit ridiculous? What has she actually done that is so terrible? Surely, we can move on and remain friends?

Sadly, when it comes to power games, there is only room for criticism, superiority and gossiping. The power-crazed bitch has won again; it was just too ridiculously easy to recruit women and manipulate a group situation.

***

Power Games Stories

I had these friends at university. The three of us had lots of fun partying together. Then, the two girls fell out over something trivial. They bitched about each other endlessly to me at every opportunity. After hearing too much, I said, *"Look, this is between you two. Sort it out, OK?"* In an instant, I was shot down. I didn't realise it at the time. Who the fuck was I not to join in and validate their feelings?

Within days, they were friends again. I thought, *Great! We can get back to having fun times again!* But I was naïve. I was 20.

The main girl said to me, *"How do you sleep at night? You must feel so guilty!"* They sort of smirked at each other.

Apparently, I had enjoyed every moment of their falling out and had encouraged the bitching. I was sick to my stomach. The girl had convinced the other one and they were now both convinced it was my fault.

What was the problem? Well, I knew too much, didn't I? I was too risky. The main girl thought, *We need to get rid of her now as she may tell the other one what was said*. I just wanted us all to get along and have fun. I had no intention of stirring anything up. I wanted to move on, but they wanted me out.

***

I notice if I don't go on Facebook and comment on a friend's status, she will refuse to comment on anything I say for weeks. My kids are ill. I've started a new job. My sister is starring in a major Hollywood film after years of knocking on doors. My husband has cancer. I'm dying of a rare disease and have weeks to live. OK, maybe not, but you get the point. Nothing from her. Nada. Instead, she comments on something that another friend says that is trivial - one of our friends gets a new haircut or paints her toenails blue, and she is literally jumping with excitement. My sin? I didn't jump in and tell her how beautiful and amazing her kids latest snaps are or how much I love her new dress. I have not been attentive enough and so now I am a crap friend and she'll ignore me. Maybe I am going nuts or maybe it is her way of claiming back some power? It seems really strange, maybe I'm a paranoid freak, but it seems to happen a lot to me. B, 39.

***

I didn't make my own birthday night out. Yes, my own. I just couldn't handle it as I was not feeling good and had just had my first baby. Now, according to my friend, I was a terrible person. This friend desperately wanted to go out and let her hair down. She was seething with outrage that I cancelled on her. I was hoping she would show some compassion, like all the love and compassion I had showered her with. But I had let her down. I had said no. I was now a disappointment in her eyes. I was no longer classed as a friend. I had not met her expectations.

I checked my emails and found she had jumped off the telephone and wrote me an abusive email. It was the first of many. More and more came in, day after day. They were very angry and she called me lots of horrible names. Every word was a personal attack. I had to cancel my email account. She used another email account and continued to send aggressive emails. I begged her to stop. I was close to calling the police as she was now threatening me. I was close to getting my parents to talk to her parents. I was at a loss – how could I get her to be reasonable? Where had my beautiful friend gone? I cried a lot. She was lost forever.

Years later, she tracked me down and apologised. She'd been going through a rough time. But I was left shaken. Her emails were rotten; I was so scared. The words still sting. These days, I have nothing but compassion for her. I forgive her completely and understand she made a terrible mistake. It was completely out of character for her to try and control me. She had been a lovely friend and I was devastated when she abused the friendship. I still miss her, but I can't allow her back into my life.

***

I've had women ostracise me for the most peculiar and trivial reasons. I don't understand where the illusion of unyieldingly loyal sisterly bonds comes from. In my experience, women have always been the quickest to judge, attack or drop. We do it all the time. We are our own worst enemies. We want to be accepted by other women, but we can't seem to accept other women! There's always a problem, always an issue. I have grown tired of it. Maybe I have been unlucky. The nurturing, loyal women are truly the minority. That kind of makes me feel sad, but maybe we need to face up to this once and for all. You know, really look at the sisterhood reality under a microscope and not through the usual rose-tinted spectacles.

***

I was stupid enough to fancy a boy at school when I was about 15. Trouble was he *had* been a boyfriend to one of my friends. I made a pathetic move on him and, of course, he rejected me. Well, not quite, but he certainly didn't pursue me. It's a chapter in my history I will always regret. It wasn't a fair move and it wasn't a clever move. If I had seen my younger self, I would have screamed at her to step back and stay away. But sadly, 15-year-olds are not always so insightful. I began to regret my actions and when I was back at school, I blurted out to my friend about my stupid mistake. We had not kissed or anything, but my intention had been dishonourable. I was deeply ashamed of allowing my hormones to take over. My friend said it was OK. Her relationship with him was now over and thanks for letting her know. She seemed happy enough to move forward and forgive me.

That very day, she then went on to tell a few other select girls in our year. The outspoken girls. The girls who love a good argument and a bit of drama! Their outrage rippled through the school. Their fury at my disgusting lust crashed into me. I was knocked off my feet.

"You are nothing but a fucking bitch, don't you know that? A fucking bitch, don't you ever forget that!"

I huddled in a ball, my arms wrapped around my legs. Hoping their words would bounce off me. I didn't want to cry, I wanted to be defiant to these girls as I knew they had made plenty of silly mistakes, but the tears fell. I was terrified. I was a mess. I'd had a rough year; there had been a lot of trauma in my personal life. I just wanted to be a normal teenage girl, but I had made a terrible error of judgement. It is hard to think straight at 15, but when you are dealing with catastrophic changes at home, it is even easier to mess up. My friend looked on, her eyes steady and cold, satisfied that I was being suitably punished.

Public humiliation would ensure my self-esteem was shattered; I wouldn't attempt to go near another boy. It was too risky for someone as repellent as me. I was utterly disgusted with myself, but deep down inside a part of me was furious at the superiority of these girls. Had they never made a stupid mistake? Had they never screwed up?

And so (of course) my friend successfully got me back. A year or so later, she was found kissing the boy I had always loved. The only boy I had adored and admired as a young girl. She knew I had loved that person with all my heart and it was the perfect revenge. It was not her mistake; it was not her misjudgement or ignorance. She knew it would break my heart and it did. I learnt quickly, if you cross a girl, if you try to walk on her territory, she will get you back. It's not OK; she's rarely cool with what you did. She will smile and hug you, she will tell you things are cool, but it is not the truth. I was on her turf and I got payback. Served me right, no doubt; it served me right for my teenage stupidity, but there was something just a little bit planned about her actions.

***

Quotations on Power

Nearly all men (or people) can stand adversity, but if you want to test a man's (or woman's) character, give them power.

Abraham Lincoln (1809-1865)

You see what power is – it is holding someone else's fear in your hand and showing it to them!

Amy Tan

We have, I fear, confused power with greatness.

Stewart L Udall

An honest person can feel no pleasure in the exercise of power over his (or her) fellow citizens.

Thomas Jefferson

The love of liberty is the love of others; the love of power is the love of ourselves.

William Hazlitt

The highest proof of virtue is to possess boundless power without abusing it.

Lord Macaulay

Bitching

Women bitch. Call it gossip, call it idle chit chat. But mostly, if the topic is about another woman, the talk will err on the side of bitchy.

"Have you seen how clean her house is? That's just unnaturally clean!"

"She has her kids in every club going. It's just ridiculous and exhausting for her and the kids!"

"I couldn't be so heartless to say it - I hate her hair dark. Lighter hair suits her so much better."

"She's out all the time; I don't know where she finds the time or the energy with a baby. I'm probably just jealous, but her social life is a bit much, isn't it? I just don't have the need these days. I think I've grown up."

"She's a skinny rake. She probably never eats a proper meal. Do you think she's OK? She probably has an eating disorder."

"Her kids are out of control. She needs to teach them some manners. I won't have them in my house again."

"Her house is gorgeous, but I bet it is so much work and she'll never afford to do much now."

Women bitch about each other to each other. It's a curious thing, bitching. We don't want other women to bitch about us. We'd be outraged and hurt if we discovered the truth of what other women may say about us behind our backs.

However, we are quick to jump in and engage in bitching with other women whenever the opportunity does arise. *"What are you saying about her?"* Or, *"Who's this we are discussing?"* Or even, *"Oh, yes. I know what you mean about her!"*

Perhaps it is survival of the fittest. It is a clever emotional strategy. If you condemn or criticise the other woman, then at least it won't hurt quite so much when she inevitably bitches about you to others. She will no doubt return the 'favour' in due course if your bitching is leaked to her or if she is equally bitchy.

Or perhaps it is simply our way of securing bonds. Albeit very rocky foundations but it is bonds nonetheless and we women have a very strong urge to seek out deep bonds by whatever means.

By bitching, we are uniting and bonding. It seems impossible to the rational mind. How can anyone possibly respect, trust and bond with a woman who bitches to you? But it happens, all the time.

Rationally, you would think a woman would conclude that a woman who bitches about others is highly likely, almost guaranteed to bitch about you, too.

Unfortunately, that is not the case. It seems many women think they are superior and immune. They believe they will never fall short or become a victim to the bitching. *It will never happen to me. She loves me! She's always nice to me! It's really just harmless gossip. She just trusts me.*

The person listening to the bitching is in a position of power. She feels wanted and trusted. It doesn't take a genius to work out that this bitching tactic works best between insecure women.

Through bitching, they feel superior to the person they condemn and they enjoy the attention, the intensity of the interaction. Both egos are massaged. The bitching woman enjoys off-loading to her friend and feels like she can trust her friend. She feels like her feelings are validated as her listening friend agrees with her and encourages her to express herself more.

They both win; the only loser is the woman that's being bitched about. She's been ripped to shreds and doesn't have a leg to stand on! But in their eyes, that's okay. They have now bonded and feel united. They now feel they can be entirely open with each other.

There is a darker side to bitching. It's gossiping on steroids.

When a woman feels powerless, she will hide her rising hostility towards another woman. They will not attack the person directly. They will attack indirectly by secretly backbiting, gossiping and bitching.

For the bitched about victim, this indirect aggression – the bitching – can lead to social rejection, ostracism and depression. Made all the worse for the victim because the bitching woman will often refuse to acknowledge her own bitchy behaviour. She will refuse to acknowledge her own jealous, competitive or angry feelings. All blame is laid on the victim – she is the scapegoat.

The victim of a bitching campaign can see the web of deception wrapped around her furiously. She will feel unable to breathe some days and have no idea how to undo all the negative press.

The person doing the bitching will refuse to admit they spun the web and they will refuse to admit they are the one doing harm.

It can be said here that women who play these bitching games do not want to be held accountable for their behaviour. The bitching woman will remain unclear about what she is doing. She will behave as though she is indifferent to the victim. The bitching woman will not name her behaviour and certainly never admit to any wrong doing. She is simply just passing on some news. She will refuse to acknowledge that her actions are unacceptable or unfair. In her eyes, the bitched about deserves her wrath.

Most women have a repertoire of impressive techniques to weaken, humiliate and ostracise other women. Bitching is just one method that works a treat! She might use silence to unnerve; she might refuse to engage the other woman. Any type of bitchy behaviour can leave us stunned and confused. Did you just imagine it or is it really happening? What makes it thoroughly confusing is within a group of women, many are unwilling to name what the bitchy woman is doing and they also seem unwilling to stop her actions. The victims are left feeling powerless and invisible. No one is aware, or are they?

Men bitch, too. Of course they do. There's a difference, though. A big difference.

Men bitch in a humorous fashion. They bitch openly and directly to the person they are mocking. They do not hide behind a veil. They do not bitch in the passive aggressive way that females do. It is much more direct.

If they think you are foolish or odd, then they are likely to tell you straight out. They are likely to joke and make fun of you. They do not bitch in the serious, dissecting a frog, hyena's devouring a dead carcass, deeply personal and all-consuming way that women can.

Got a dodgy new haircut? A man is likely to say something cheeky to his male friend, directly – there and then in the present moment. He is very unlikely to smile and say you look beautiful. And then the next day say to another friend, *"He looks truly awful."*

The difference may be because women walk on egg shells within their female friendships. They are desperately trying to keep their 'precious' friendships alive.

Men treat their friendships like an old football. They kick it around and say what they want.

In man world, very few things are taken personally. It's just not as important - they say things to each other and their words are not analysed to within an inch of their life. They don't tend to stew over what they say to each other. Men are a lot more relaxed with each other as a result. They don't expect so much from each other, they don't need each other. There is not great importance placed on each other pulling their emotional weight. Things with men are easier.

Meet any group of men and listen to their relaxed conversations. If a man started bitching to his male friends in the aggressive, cutting way like a woman can, his friends would look at their friend curiously. *"Is everything alright, mate? You um...don't seem too happy."* Or, *"Shut up! He's your mate. Give him a break. I don't want to hear any more of your negative crap, alright?"* Or even, *"I totally disagree with you. He's a good mate of mine."*

It is much fairer with men. If they are not happy, they tell you. If they think you are being too harsh, they will tell you. If they think you're an idiot, you'll know soon enough as they will tell you.

There's very little bullshit. Things are frank, not fake. Eggs are well and truly smashed. You'll probably never truly know how a woman feels about you.

Women know that every word, every action is judged by other women. They know they can be burnt at the stake at a moment's notice if they step out of line, if they upset the status quo. Thanks to the spread of bitching, everyone they know can turn cold. It can feel like they have stepped into the Arctic Circle.

And so, in this suffocating and controlling vacuum that is female friendship, women often bitch to other women behind closed doors.

Bitching is a desperate attempt to gain some personal power over the unpredictable and fragile nature of female friendships.

A woman cannot risk being as direct as a man with her friends. She would risk rejection and ostracism. Women struggle to take another female's disagreement on the chin. It is far safer for women to have some trusted confidants than being direct with the very women who are flustering her feathers.

If you think a woman is bitching about you, but you're not too sure, it may be a good idea to consider whether your 'friend' had a healthy relationship with her mother.

What was her mother actually like? Was her mother bitchy? Was her mother domineering and powerful? If the answer is yes to any of these questions, you could have a 'Monkey see, monkey do' case on your hands.

It takes an incredibly strong woman to retrain her brain and say to herself, *My mum was a critical, domineering woman. I'm breaking this habit! I want to be fairer and be much more understanding of the people in my life!*

Most women will naturally behave how their mothers behaved. We will copy our master and bitch because it was what we witnessed as young girls or we will bitch because we are trying to claw back some control.

Our mothers' bitchy habits do leave a mark on our character. It is up to us as adults to recognise our poor behaviour and understand *why* we bitch.

Sadly, honest and open reflections about our bitching habits are quite a rare accordance due to the emotional pain involved. It is far easier to project the anger and frustration of our mothering at other women. Other women are an easier target.

***

Bitching Stories

I know women bitch about me. I know because I bitch, too. We all do, some more than others, of course. Women are always very nice to your face, but you just know they don't really rate you.

In high school it really peaks. The girls are on a bitching frenzy. They don't even try to hide their displeasure in seeing you. They do all the passive aggressive behaviour possible. It's a wonder any girl leaves school with her self-esteem still intact. I'd really just prefer a kick or a punch!

I'd love to tell women that it gets better with age, but it really doesn't. If you look around and listen, you can see the bitching is still going on. The women just get more clever and manipulative with their methods. It can be harder to detect, but it's there undercover. M, 25.

***

I moved to a different country and was introduced to a group of women. Things were going well enough, everyone was pleasant, but the full chemistry of the group changed when another woman (who I initially had introduced!) joined the group.

I don't know how it happens, but just one person can alter the full group with her energy. She needed to be in control, being part of our group wasn't enough. She wanted to be the central person.

When I was in a position of weakness – I had some serious health problems (I don't wish to burden the reader with a list of health issues, but let's just say it was a terrible time full of blood tests, stress and worry) just before birth and post-baby - she made herself indispensable to them. Not to me – the person who has just had a baby, the person with no family in Australia, the person in and out of hospital – nope, she made herself available to the other women in my life. I was after all useless and often unable to get out of the house. To add insult to my poor physical health, I also became very depressed. It wasn't a pretty sight. Perhaps I would have stayed away from me also. Of course, I tried to hide it all, but I couldn't get out of the house most days.

In a way, I guess I no longer existed. I was no longer attending coffee mornings or 'making an effort'. The former 'sociable' Alana seized to exist. She and another woman she had 'recruited' began to drop my name from invites. Before I knew it, I was dropped from a friend's baby shower (I think everyone in that town was invited but me), girls' nights out, and birthday parties. They said I wouldn't make the effort to come anyway, so why bother asking me. Before I got ill, I was the person organising a lot of the events. It was quite amazing how she managed to alter people's perception of me. How she managed to erase me and how no one really noticed that I was missing.

Growing more and more depressed, hopeless and more outraged, I did try to clear my name by exposing the truth. I tried to expose her. I wrote an email reply to a woman who had after some time asked me where the hell I was. But it was impossible to expose her without coming across as a pathetic, paranoid bitch. It was impossible to explain how cruel she could be. It was impossible to explain how this woman had hurt people before me, women who were good people and she would hurt people again. I tried to warn her, but it was useless. Perhaps it really was my entire fault and I was imagining everything? Perhaps if I had made more of an effort?

In the end, I gave up. I took a huge step sideways. There was little point in trying to convince the other women of my innocence. I did try to undo the damage, but it was impossible - her smear campaign had worked. I was too hurt that they valued this manipulative woman. But they did. They considered her reliable, sociable, fun and loyal. Everything I had could not compare to her. I had become the isolated, weird one. They didn't rate me as a person. They didn't want to hear the inconvenient truth. They saw me as a delusional trouble maker. Her bitching had worked wonders. I had to swallow my pride and move on. I wish I'd said nothing, kept quiet, not tried to protest, not tried to recruit some support from my 'friends'. I've learned a valuable lesson and it is one I shall never forget; people believe what suits them.

***

One woman bitched so much about me that my friend never invited me to her wedding. I don't know how or why this woman managed to get such a hold on my friend, but she did. She turned them all against me. I was understandably confused and distraught. I don't think I can ever forgive my friends as they were so easily swayed by this woman. They are all still friends. I am glad to be free, though. I don't have to be caught up in the bitching anymore. It is a relief, but it was so painful and horrible at first. The injustice of it all made me ill. I had stomach ulcers for months! C, 42.

***

I find it really hard to trust women. I've had so many bad experiences. They just seem unnaturally quick to point the finger and find fault in other women, but never with themselves. They are the same with men, of course; women like to change men and improve them. Well, guys, we women don't get off lightly either! Women believe they are in the right and they are already perfect and don't need to change. But with women, we don't even try to accept each other's flaws or change them, we very often just criticise each other. I think we forgive men a lot more. I think we always give men chances (often when we really shouldn't!) but we very rarely give a female friend more than one chance.

***

Quotations on Bitching

Until you can prove yourself perfect, you cannot put others down for their imperfections.

Unknown

I'd rather be hated for who I am, than loved for who I am not.

Unknown

No one can make you feel inferior without your consent.

Eleanore Roosevelt

Bullying behaviour is an obnoxious way for someone with a severe inferiority complex to feel bigger than they are.

C.Youste

I don't hate the haters, they're my biggest fans.

Unknown

A doubtful friend is worse than a certain enemy. Let a man be one thing or the other, and we then know how to meet him.

Aesop

Speak well of your friend, of your enemy say nothing.

Unknown

Nothing is as dangerous as an ignorant friend; a wise enemy is to be preferred.

Jean de La Fontaine

We will remember not the words of our enemies, but the silence of our friends.

Unknown

You have enemies? Good. That means you've stood up for something, sometime in your life!

Unknown

Competition

Just like some men, some women are competitive. Some women will compete almost instinctively with other women.

Notice a woman getting ready to go out. She will ensure her necklace perfectly matches her dress, or her shoes are the latest fashion. This preening is not for a man's benefit. He is highly unlikely to notice. But other women will always notice her and judge her. Every woman knows this.

Women compete with each other all the time and over the most surreal things. It starts with who has the prettiest dress at a birthday party when they are five and progresses to who has the most advanced, beautiful baby or largest home at thirty-five.

"Is your baby walking yet? No? My baby was walking at 10 months. They are all different. Don't worry about it."

"Have you seen the latest must-have hand bag? All the WAGS have one. I am waiting for mine to arrive today."

"You're wearing that dress, again. It is lovely, though."

"Are you ready for the interview? I'm just going to try and wing it. It can't be that hard to get this job as we are both going for it."

"I have the best husband ever! He treats me like a princess every day of my life! We can't keep our hands off each other. I have the most amazing sex life, you know."

"I've lost so much weight. How much have you lost"

"We are going to buy land and hopefully make a profit. Our own mini empire of land purchases. We are in such a good position these days; it makes sense to invest our money. Do you not get a bit sick of renting? Does this rental not depress you?"

If any of these comments leave you feeling a little cold and uneasy, you're not alone.

Competition from other women is designed to give you an emotional wobble. It is designed to catch you off guard and make you feel insecure and not quite up to scratch. That way, the competitive woman has an emotional head start.

She is always seeking to lead the way and be in control. You are often left at the starting line, staring at her perfectly defined buttocks.

It's a curious thing why women feel the need to be competitive of each other. It would be simpler if they could treat other women as their equals or allies. Surely, we have enough to fight for already without fighting against each other?

But the thing about competitive women is they believe they have to be superior to you and me. They are also hugely insecure and need to keep reaffirming their own self-worth in this world. It's a double whammy of psychological issues directed at you.

Most competitive women have a touch of narcissism in their character. It's not all bad news; narcissists gave the world art, business, inventions, science, sports and anything remotely competitive.

However, these women somehow make a competitive game out of giving birth, raising kids, dressing themselves, their health, their homes, their jobs, their husbands, their investments.

These women have a very strong desire to impress you and be exceptional. They never want to be ordinary in life.

Whilst a little narcissism is fabulous for humanity, as it encourages people to be the best, it can be hugely frustrating in your own personal life.

The competitive woman doesn't seem to want to benefit humanity and be remembered for her greatness; instead, she is merely competing with you.

She is telling you - your kitchen is nice, but is that the cheapest range?

She is telling you - your children simply must get into the latest club or they will be sporting failures.

She is telling you - she cooks for her husband every night and it is a pleasure to cook for such a beautiful and romantic man.

Your frozen pizza seems pathetic in comparison!

In fact, your life seems rather ordinary in comparison.

Sigh.

You smile and try to feel pleased for her, but something deep inside tells you she is trying to make you feel worthless. She makes you feel like your life is second rate, your choices are not so clever, and your lifestyle is rather stale in comparison.

A competitive woman is not thinking about your feelings, your thoughts or your needs. She is purely motivated and consumed by her own desires.

She is not trying to motivate you or encourage you to improve your life, she is merely boasting about her glossy life.

She is obsessively concerned about her status and power in the world.

At the very root of her behaviour – she is desperate for your admiration. She is desperate for your approval. It can be hard to see over her huge ego, though. And she just seems a little bit too obnoxious.

But you, of course, try to let her remarks wash over you. Maybe she is right; maybe your new carpet is cheap and won't last long with three kids? Maybe she's just honest; your other friends are deceiving you?

Or maybe she is someone who enjoys undermining you and leaving you feeling like a worthless loser?

Competition between women is a game with no winners. She will always be looking behind her back and wondering how far ahead she is. You will always be desperately trying to keep up with her.

Women get themselves into debt just to ensure they have a good enough car for the school drop off. Women get themselves into financial strife just to ensure they have all the gadgets and furnishings that their friend has. Women get themselves into an exhausting logistical pickle just to ensure their kids have a place in every after school club, every sport available to them.

You'll never truly impress your competitive friend. She'll always be ahead of the game anyway. Why do it to yourself emotionally, financially, physically?

It's not a healthy friendship; it is a competitive dual.

Throw out your running shoes and live your own life – your way, on your terms. What is important to her – does not need to be important to you.

***

Competition Stories

I had a friend who was always asking me about what my baby was eating, if he was talking yet, what he was saying. She never wasted a chance to tell me how her daughter was advanced. I wanted to scream that all babies are different, but this was a competitive game she couldn't resist having with me. L, 32.

***

You go out with a gaggle of girls on a night out and they all size each other up a bit. It is done in a very subtle way, but if you pay attention, you can see the girls looking you up and down and making snap judgements on their female competition for the night. Often the prettiest girl is given the least compliments. The fat girl is always told she looks amazing. The skinny girl doesn't need a compliment – oh, but she probably does! We are all women after all. We all want to be told we are beautiful! K, 26.

***

She would walk into my house and I could see her looking at my furniture, how tidy my house was, how clean it was. I knew my home was never going to be as *show home perfect* as her home and I stopped trying, but I could see the truth in her eyes - her superiority mixed with insecurity. It was really weird. She then tried to hide her feelings and would look all warmly at me and smile. I don't know why I let her in my house, but she always warmed up. It was just at the beginning; she was sizing up my environment and comparing us.

***

We both had babies at the same time. She was naturally a bit slimmer than me and, of course, her baby weight came off easily for her. I was happy for her and congratulated her. When I finally lost weight and I was chuffed to feel healthy again, she never said a thing. I was not her friend, I was her competition. There is a difference. A, 30.

I was out with a group of friends, a mix of couples. I picked up that the wife sitting across from me in our group didn't like the look of me one little bit. She'd never met me before, but she wasn't interested in speaking to me. I tried to be friendly and ask her about herself, but she gave short, sharp answers. She knew I was a mum, and yet she spent most of the evening talking about her career. For some bizarre reason, instead of seeing me as a potential mate, I was competition. She was a chubby girl. The reason I tell you this pointless information is because she commented on my weight in the most ridiculous way. Please do note I'm a healthy UK size 10.

As the evening went on, I excused myself and said I was off to powder my nose. She looked me up and down before saying,

"I thought you were going to the toilet to be sick again."

Taken aback and dumbfounded, I said, *"Why?"*

*"I thought you **had** to be anorexic."* She smiled sweetly before turning away from me.

Speechless. *What?! What a strange thing to say. Help. Breathe, Alana, just breathe. Just walk away.*

***

Mums compete with each other. Mums can even attack other mums. Mums who are insecure will struggle to share your joy. Your pride and love for your family will make her uncomfortable. Their inferiority complex is so strong they will see you as competition. They'll blame you for trying to make them feel inferior. Their view of who you are and who they are as mums is distorted. Instead of sharing in your joy of motherhood, they feel angry, jealous and insecure. Their inferiority complex is their own issue, but they project it onto you, and blame you entirely for how they feel deep inside. They refuse to own and fix their own negative feelings; it's your fault they feel inferior. A friendship becomes nothing more than a pathetic competition. Who will be the best mum? Oh, please stop this madness! Stop throwing crap at other mums as they have enough crap and sick to clean up as it is.

***

Quotes on Competition

Competing with yourself makes you better. Competing with others makes you bitter.

Unknown

Never compete with someone who has nothing to lose.

Baltasar Gracián

Real learning comes about when the competitive spirit has ceased.

Jiddu Krishnamurti

Life is one race I never want to win; I'd rather stroll around enjoying the scenery.

Aditya Chandra

Nobody's going to win all the time. On the highway of life you can't always be in the fast lane.

Haruki Murakami

If any of my competitors were drowning, I'd stick a hose in their mouth.

Ray Kroc

Never letting the competition define you. Instead, you have to define yourself based on a point of view you care deeply about.

Tom Chappel

My grandfather once told me that there are two kinds of people: those who work and those who take the credit. He told me to try to be in the first group; there was less competition there.

Indira Gandhi

The Harsh Truths

We have some disturbing truths that we as females must now accept. Ignoring or minimising these truths will serve us no purpose.

The only way to ensure healthier female friendships in your future is to fully acknowledge the dark side of feminine relations.

We can avoid future problems through knowledge and awareness. You won't be bulletproof, but at least you can be conscious and able to see the warning signs early on.

We have seen how women can use a dazzling range of tactics to manipulate, control, contort and please themselves.

My personal interpretation is that some women can use intricate behaviours on each other that are obscure, cryptic, puzzling, concealed, cruel and unfair.

My belief is that these convoluted behaviours are rampant in *some* female circles. If you are living and breathing on this planet, it pays to be conscious of these negative behaviours. It is surely wise to be fully aware of our feminine reality than to live in blissful ignorance.

I am not trying to mislead you. This is our reality, this is our truth. Female inhumanity is an actuality. It can and does exist within some women.

But what are the cold hard truths? What are the important behaviours we all need to be aware of? What are the behaviours we need to open our eyes to in order to safeguard our own mental health, spirits and sense of self?

There are specific behaviours that some women display that, if ignored, will cause you great hurt and upheaval. It is wise to fully acknowledge that sometimes women can display inhumanity towards other women in the most subtle or blatant ways.

The cold hard truth hurts. It goes against the widely held belief that all women are fairy godmothers. It goes against our belief that all women are nurturing, fair and kind.

But with truth comes insight and knowledge. And with this knowledge, you will gain awareness and the ability to protect yourself from future hurt.

So let's take a closer look at the behaviours that are most frequently occurring amongst some women. Let's become fully conscious of these behaviours now to safeguard our own personal happiness.

Women prefer to exist in cliques or dyads.

It is safer for women to exist in groups or a pair. In these groups, women will perfect the act of banishing/rejecting/bitching about other women who they perceive to be a threat to their inner circle. This power actually keeps everyone in line and withholds the status quo of the group. No one wants to be the next target! Women often renew and re-establish their bonds within a group through ostracising and criticising other women. Yes, really!

Women are often purposely blind to bullies.

A woman is usually reluctant to stand up to a bully. In fact, they often fail to even notice a bully exists in their social circle. Simply put, to interrogate a bully would be a risky strategy. Women are much more likely to let go of their morals and principles to ensure they remain securely nestled in a group. They know that by reprimanding a 'queen bee', they also risk social rejection. Too much is at stake. It is safer to ignore the bullying or pretend to be unaware. It is easier to 'turn a blind eye'. She's nice to me after all!

Women refuse to acknowledge their own negative feelings.

Women are often unwilling to acknowledge their own competitive, angry or jealous feelings. It is socially unacceptable for women to possess such emotions. The trouble with this ignorance and refusal to own the emotion is that hostile feelings towards other women fester and their angry feelings are rarely resolved. Deep seated ill-will, bitterness and rancour can result from the most minor disagreements and situations.

Women desire mothering.

It is a widely held belief that it is only men who enjoy mothering. All women enjoy mothering, too! However men do not expect mothering from their male friends. That's the big difference. Unconsciously, women expect mothering from their female friends. Women are therefore emotional needy and greedy with each other. There is an unnatural dependence on emotional grooming. This intensity creates an illusion of closeness with women you barely know.

It's instant intimacy and it is available to women quickly and easily as they crave it back from you!

Women are human beings.

Women are normal, healthy human beings who are able to feel jealousy, envy, anger, bitterness, aggression, competition. These are all very normal human emotions. Due to social pressures, women 'pretend' to always be fair and good people. But, of course, this is an unrealistic and impossible standard to maintain. It is perhaps time to challenge the simple notion that all women are kind and gentle people. Women are capable of dominating and wounding. They are capable of shocking cruelty towards other women, children and men. It is not simply men who can be inhumane. Women are human beings. And like all humans, they have profound emotional limitations.

Women have power over each other.

The power that women bestow upon each other is usually hidden well from the world and from men. But women do exercise power over each other. A woman's ability to control, manipulate and hurt other women is powerful and often stunning. Women are often treated as second class citizens, but women to women, we are equal and ultimately our inhumanity to each other can be painful and shocking.

Women struggle to embrace difference.

To women in groups or dyads – sameness and conforming to the group's status quo is essential. A difference of opinion, a different life style, a different style of dressing, a life change – it can all mean rejection to a woman. For a woman to survive in any group, she must leave her independent thoughts and diversity at the door. She must conform; she must be neutral and agreeable. Women are fearful of difference, of uniqueness. Diversity in a group threatens them. Women know being different is too risky – it could mean banishment. It is safer to just 'fit in' and order what everyone else is drinking. It is safer to just smile, nod and agree.

Women struggle to relate when threatened.

A woman relates best when she does not feel threatened by a 'brighter light'. She can only emotionally groom when she feels she is in a position of power. It is impossible for her to relate and feel compassion for a woman who threatens her sense of self. The only time a woman will 'relate' to a brighter light is when the brighter light can give her improved social status or benefit her in some way. Otherwise, a woman will feel happier mothering and bonding with a lesser light or someone who she is sure is her equal.

Indirect aggression is a woman's weapon.

Men are often too direct, women are often too indirect. The range of indirect aggressions is mind boggling. She can shame, whisper, slander, ostracise, banish, cut you dead, give dirty looks, influence your friends and her friends, befriend your enemies, gossip, bitch, back bite, snarl, smirk, undermine, freeze you out, ignore you, refuse to engage with you just to name just a few! The passive aggressive techniques are long and endless.

The trouble with indirect aggression? It is like being kicked in the stomach by an invisible person. You know it's happening, it feels awful, but it's almost impossible to pinpoint or name what is happening. The aggressor would never acknowledge her behaviour anyway.

If a man does not like you – he will generally let you know directly. A fist will come at your face or he will tell you directly why he dislikes you. It is direct! When men are angry, they get physical, they start world wars, they invade countries, they intimidate you by their very presence or they tell you straight out that you're an idiot. A man's aggression is powerful, primal, sometimes violent and always forthright. Men are the kings of direct aggression. It's often messy, it often results in injury, but often it is over quickly. Often there are no grudges held if a resolution can be achieved. The aggression is fast, it's direct and it's not usually emotionally complicated.

If you're a man, you nurse your sore eye and feel sorry for yourself. But you are under no illusions. You understand how the man who was aggressive feels about you. You understand his motives and most likely you both move on quickly, a little embarrassed, no doubt.

In comparison, if you are a victim of indirect aggression, you'll feel confused, anxious, upset and uncomfortable. Haunted by an invisible force – rather like a taunting ghost. The aggression follows you all over and makes you miserable to the core. You feel on edge, when will she stop? You start to blame yourself – *If this woman hates me so much, then I must be a terrible person.*

Indirect aggression is a soup that stews on and on for years. It endlessly chips away at a woman's sense of self. Eroding her self-worth day in, day out. You will probably never have a bruised eye, but you will have a bruised ego, a wounded spirit and low self-confidence. You won't need to nurse a bleeding cut or pay for some new teeth, but you will need to repair and nurture your hurt soul. Women are the masters of indirect aggression.

Women hold onto grudges.

If there is anything a woman can hold onto tightly and with passion, it is a grudge. Some women must feel very heavy inside; every day, for years, they carry around with them grudges.

"Sally didn't come to my engagement party. What a bitch. I would have moved mountains to go to her event. I mean she was pregnant and all, but come on. If she really valued me, she'd have wiped away her morning sickness stains and got herself to my party!"

I wish I was joking. But this thought process is surprisingly common.

Instead of the 'wronged' woman 'putting herself into her friend's shoes' and trying to understand, she pouts and holds a grudge. She cannot comprehend why her friend was unable to put her needs or desires first. It is another example of a woman expecting to be number one priority no matter what's going on in the other person's life.

I wish I could say it gets better as we mature through life, but sadly, even retired women are known to hold grudges that span generations of families. Tiny misunderstandings and little mistakes that happened years before can be blown up into catastrophic events.

Whether your actions or words were ridiculously thoughtless or unintentionally hurtful, the 'wronged' woman will find she cannot help her silent seething. It becomes part of her chemistry. Part of her character.

Why do some women hold onto grudges with such fearsome determination? Why can't they just let go and accept sometimes things don't work out as planned?

In some way, they feel you have crossed them. You have disappointed them or let them down. They expected more from you. Somehow it makes sense to hold on to their anger. The 'wronged' woman thinks it will punish you, but holding onto bitterness only tends to hurt them.

Let's put ourselves into their shoes (even if they fail to do that for us) for a moment.

These women are often not able to think logically. Their response to upset is rather childlike. Instead of communicating with us, they push the hurt to the side. It is not dealt with. They think we don't care. Instead of dealing with the upset straightaway, they pretend everything is fine. The wrong-doer can often have no idea. The wrong-doer is often given no opportunity to make amends.

Women hate being wrong.

Are women ever in the wrong or do they believe they can change the other person's mind?

Do they always find a way of twisting a story to look like the victim?

Do they find it hard to apologise, admit they are wrong and start over - and are they more likely to desperately grabble for what you did wrong to them - instead of just owning their own bad behaviour and saying sorry?

Yes. Yes. Yes!

Women find it unbearable and impossible to be wrong. They'd rather lose a friend than admit they have been ridiculously wrong. They'd rather blame the person they hurt, than apologise for hurting them.

Women think they are superior friends.

Women are not the friends they think they are. Women are not the intimacy experts they like to believe they are. They mess up and hurt people just as much as a man can. Women can be surprisingly insensitive to each other.

They are not quick to stand up and support a friend. First, they must be sure that it is safe to do so. How will their actions actually upset their own life? This is often considered. They do not go down in a blaze of flames and burn their own bridges for the sake of supporting a girlfriend who has been hurt. They do not have the all consuming passion and loyalty for each other. Often they say and do nothing.

And yet they believe they are superior, perfect friends.

***

The truth hurts, but how can we protect ourselves from these behaviours?

The above attributes are prevalent in some female circles. Is it now time to step into the light instead of darting around in the shadows afraid to speak out about these behaviours? I think so.

There is no denying, a woman's inhumanity can cripple and stun other women.

How can we best guard ourselves against other women who are negative forces in our life? How can we defend ourselves and shield our precious spirits from habitually being trodden on by careless or apathetic women?

Simply put, you have the answer in your hands.

This book gives you knowledge to open up your mind and eyes to what is actually going on in your office, your college, your home.

This book gives you the opportunity to now become fully conscious of how women can conduct themselves. It is imperative to remain mindful and vigilant.

It is pointless to pretend all is rosy with all the women that you know. Sometimes the garden can be torn to shreds at a moment's notice and it is vital as women that we recognise the damage we can do to each other.

Furthermore, I will explain in the next chapter how to only allow positive, healthy women into your life. You will see that, by acknowledging that negative women and their games exist and by blocking out the negative women, you can protect yourself from future pain.

Finding Positive Women

In this book we have discovered the negative behaviours that some women can possess and effortlessly implement within their female friendships. I hope you feel more aware and able to 'protect' yourself from the negative women who conduct these behaviours.

I also hope you feel more emphatic and ready to understand why a friend may be behaving badly towards you. It is easier to let go and not take things to heart when you truly understand what could lie beneath a woman's behaviour.

It's not always easy to find compassion for a friend or equally know when to move on from a friend, but if you understand her personal motivations, her agenda or what is actually driving her behaviour, you are more likely to make good judgements.

It can hurt to realise that your own personal contentment may be entirely unimportant to her. It can be disappointing to discover that she may not have your best interest at heart. It is also confronting to realise that some women struggle with the basic concept of what friendship means in a wider context. It can be hurtful to discover that our friend may not be too concerned about loyalty and fairness – their own needs and desires dominate the relationship.

The harsh reality can hurt; some people truly are impossible to navigate, but it's surely best to know the truth. We are adults; we can choose to take the truth on board and process the information to improve our personal life.

As we have seen, in order to survive within female friendships, we must self-regulate, speak cautiously and neutrally.

A woman has to learn how to flatter her female friends. She must learn quickly how to manipulate, agree and appease other women. It is thoroughly exhausting.

But does it have to be like this?

Can't women have healthy, direct and authentic friendships?

Can't we leave all the complicated games behind?

Can't we enjoy an easy going and good-humoured friendship?

I think it is possible.

Despite often feeling worn out by the emotional games, I still believe in a thing called 'Friendship'. But I have had to learn some tough lessons along the way.

•I have discovered that in order to stay emotionally safe, I have to keep my guard up. Many times I have been too trusting, too open, and far too needy. Sadly, some women take advantage and use my vulnerability against me.

•I have discovered and accepted that I cannot expect unconditional love. I expected to gain far too much from females. That was a big mistake. Women are only human after all. I expected sisterly bonds that were eternally loyal; I expected unconditional love no matter how stupidly I behaved. This was an impossible sisterhood ideal. I was sold the dream and I believed it. I never had a sister, so perhaps I craved her.

•It is actually more likely that I will receive envy, competition, indifference, fair-weathered friendship, jealousy, anger, distance, silence, rejection and disinterest from women. It is a challenge to find women who truly do love me.

•It is easy to meet people but difficult to make secure connections. The trouble is, you are not allowed many mistakes with women. They do not love you warts and all. Women find it difficult to move on and forgive. Often women end their friendships abruptly and without much opportunity to sort out differences.

•I can't expect to gel or connect with every woman. Some women will never like me no matter how agreeable I am with them. I must remember to walk away. Some women will just not like the look of me, what I stand for, how I parent or the clothes I own. Some women will dislike me without ever truly getting to know me. All I can do is move on and hope that the next female gives me a chance.

•Women are not angels, but they are not devils. They are human beings. They have limitations.

•Women are often scared to speak the truth. The reality is women would rather keep quiet and not upset anyone. But sometimes saying and doing nothing allows crappy things to go on. But most women think to themselves, *Ah, but if I say something, how will my words impact my own life?*

•Women do have the capacity to comfort and love other women. But first, they must learn to love themselves.

Armed with these lessons, I have often wondered where are these authentic women who are capable of loving other women with all their heart. Where are the women who are willing to forgive and able to see the big picture?

"OK, she drank too much vodka and was sick on my shoes, made a tit of herself, but let's face it, most of the time she is great. That's life! Sometimes nights out aren't how we expected them to be; it is not the end of the world. She is a nutter sometimes, but most of the time she's good person."

When women are secure, content people, they make beautiful, cherished friends to each other. Secure friends don't feel inferior; they don't take themselves so seriously. Mistakes happen. People mess up. Secure friends don't have a need to present the perfect image. Life is about messy, but real, connections.

We all desire friendship. It is our natural desire to hope for emotionally enriching connections. But this desire can mean we lose sight of what is actually healthy for us. We can ignore or minimise our friend's hurtful behaviour because our natural need for love, acceptance and approval is all consuming. This is incredibly common. It happens all the time.

We desire and need friends in our life. Life would be very dull without friends. But, of course, sometimes we are blinded by a person's apparent acceptance of us and unknowingly, we welcome the enemy into our world with open arms.

This is OK, this is normal. Let's not panic. We live and we learn from our mistakes. We can learn from our willingness to accept anyone and everyone. We just need to learn to be *a bit* more discerning!

Do you want to know the truth about me? As I am sure you will know, I am a woman and just like you, I have been hurt many times by many women and I have no doubt in my mind that I have also hurt and let down many women..

But something about me never changes.

I need ***meaningful connections*** to feel satisfied in my personal relations.

The reality is connections can take a long time to catch light and blaze in all their glory. Sometimes connections will never catch fire no matter how much you try. Sometimes connections simply fizzle out.

It is easy to meet people, but difficult and time-consuming to make real and healthy connections with people. It takes lots of time and patience. It also takes a healthy dose of perception and experience to be able to see the positive women and avoid the negative.

I am someone who would much rather have a handful of close, intimates - safe and warm in their love and acceptance - truly bliss. I usually feel rather lost and lonely in a huge crowd of chattering strangers.

But like most people, there are times when I do need to make new friends or new women inevitably come into my life. With this in mind, it pays to be 'aware' of who is actually a potential friend. It pays to keep our eyes wide open and our ears fine-tuned! Who truly has friendship potential and which women will potentially behave badly once they are invited into our inner sanction?

This final chapter is designed to help you concentrate on getting *more* of the positive women into your world. The questions are designed to root out the negative women and plant the positive women into your daily life.

The negative women will become blatantly obvious to you – no longer can they hide from your crystal clear perception! Only the positive, healthy women can stay put and grow with you.

I hope with this chapter you can really 'see' what is going on around you with the women in your life. Wouldn't it be fantastic to really know who is a friend or who has the potential to become a beautiful friend? Why invest energy and love on women who don't particularly like you?

How do you plant the positive women and root out the negative?

The trick is to be ruthlessly upfront and honest with yourself.

There are some very important questions you need to ask yourself. Take your time and be honest with yourself.

With total honestly, you can be assured you will encourage only the healthy friendships to grow. The darker, negative relationships cannot thrive in your glowing, content world. They will feel endlessly frustrated by you.

Here are the all-important questions to discover if you have a positive or negative friend in your life. Take a moment to really consider each question.

•Can you turn down an invite and know this is acceptable to them? They respect you have your own life and can't make every event or want to! They will not hold a grudge or freeze you out. This is a deal breaker. Many friendships have shattered the minute a person has refused an invite or been unable to attend. Can you comfortably make your apologies and say no to a friend? Or are you made to feel like an unsatisfactory friend? Is the guilt laid on you just too unbearable that you always feel obligated to say yes?

•Can you laugh in their company? You laugh so hard you cry? If you can't laugh with your friends, then who can you laugh with? Ask yourself honestly – is there plenty of light-hearted fun, good will and merry times had? Or is it all a bit fixed, stern, rigid, reserved or polite? If you want to, you should be able to throw your hands up in the air, laugh loudly, make ridiculous, but amusing, comments, and chuckle at how absurd life is together. Life can be tough; we all need friends who act as a buffer and can make us smile.

•Do they celebrate your differences? Are they interested in your insights, your uniqueness? They don't scorn or judge or criticize you. We are all different and friends value individuality. They admire uniqueness. Or are you made to feel like you need to curb your enthusiasm? Are you made to feel like you need to tone your personality down to 'fit in' and not rock the status quo?

•Do they ever make you feel undervalued or inferior? You should feel comfortable around them. They don't undermine you or mock you unfairly. Are you ever made to feel second rate? Do they behave superior to you and make you feel like your life is inferior? Do they undermine what you say or mock your life choices?

•Are they real people? They have flaws and are open about their imperfections? They expect and know you are not perfect either and still like you. Friendship cannot be built on fake foundations. Friendship can only be built on honest foundations. They have nothing to hide from you. They are willing to share their past and life lessons. They know they sometimes mess up and get things wrong, but equally, they know you are the same. It is healthy to have some personality flaws; it is unnatural to be squeaky clean and perfect.

•Do they protect your name? They have your back. If someone is speaking ill of you they will quickly correct the person or at least disagree entirely and insist you are a good person with a good heart. A good friend will always have your back. She will never gossip about you in a negative manner, slander your name or allow someone else to partake in unfair representation. She will always protect your reputation and ensure any misrepresentation is corrected.

•Do they appreciate you as an individual person? They respect your space, your choices, and your path? They may disagree with you, but they always respect you. Respect is an important quality in friendship. Without respect, friendship cannot blossom. Any fool can criticise, mock and condemn you - that's easy. It takes a special friend to respect and admire your choices when everyone else is negative or indifferent.

•They want you to be happy and content in life? Even if your choices do not benefit them. Your personal happiness is important to them. A friend wants you to be happy. They can put themselves in your shoes and consider how you truly feel. They can appreciate your situation for what it is. A friend will want you to be happy even if it means they lose you. This self-less act is friendship. She does not try to control you or hold you hostage emotionally. She respects you and ultimately wants to see you smile.

•Do you feel your friend is your cheerleader in life? She is always cheering you on and telling you to give things a go. She believes in you and thinks you can achieve anything you set your mind on. A friend will believe in your ability to achieve your goals. They encourage you to progress in your life. She is not fearful of change in your life. She feels secure and wants you to be content.

•They fill you in and include you in group conversations? She always wants you to feel comfortable and secure. This sounds little, but it can mean a lot. Many of us have sat listening to our friend chat to another friend about someone who we have never met. We smile politely, but inside we feel invisible. A friend will try her best to include you and reassure you. She cares enough about you to ensure you are comfortable.

•Is she delighted to be with you or does she expect to see you a lot? In some friendships, there are large obligations or expectations over your head. It is far healthier if she respects you have boundaries and your own life to lead. If she sees you, she is pleased, but if not, she won't harbour a grudge.

•Is she positive about the changes you make in your life? She is open and positive about any changes you make to improve your life. She knows where she ends and you begin. She has her own life to make changes if she pleases and respects you may need to do the same.

•Does she ask you how you are feeling about things? She is curious about how you feel about important issues, what you think matters to her and she respects your opinion. She is also concerned about your emotional health. She keeps a check on that and checks on how content you feel deep down.

•Does she listen to your response? Is she responsive? Many friends ask how you are, but many don't really listen or pay close attention to your answer or body language. A friend will pick up on your feelings, whether it is your disconnection or your blissful contentment, and respond to your feelings.

•Can you be yourself? Do you feel totally relaxed in her company? Do you enjoy each other's company? If you can't relax in a friend's company and be who you are, then this is far from a friendship. We should feel like our friend is not judging our words, our choices, our clothes, our homes. She is here to see you; she should not be inspecting you, your home, your children, your fridge or your bathroom.

•Can you make a fool of yourself? Make stupid mistakes? If she is a friend, she will always see the good in you. She will always remind you that you are a good person and she has also made mistakes in life! She won't use your mistakes as an opportunity to feel superior or beat you up.

•Is she actually interested in you as a person? Some people are not interested at all. Some people are wonderful conversationalists, but in reality, they only want to talk about themselves. This can be exhausting as the relationship is completely unbalanced and focused on her. Ideally, it should be equal. You should be interested in her life and she should be interested in your life. How often do they actually ask - How are you doing? And most importantly - do they wait for your answer? You'll be amazed how frequently people ask this and how often they have stopped listening as soon as they have asked.

•Does she encourage you to follow your dreams? A secure friend will always tell you to go after your dreams and not to look back. An insecure friend will shy away from your dreams. They will make her feel anxious. She could also feel jealous and competitive. If she is negative about your dreams, she is likely to behave indifferent, uninterested and detached. That's your big, fat clue! If you feel wary of discussing your dreams to a friend, your instinct already knows deep down. Your instinct knows that your friend will not be interested.

And last, but by no means least, consider this.

•Are they trustworthy – keeping their lips sealed about your personal business? Do you feel like you have to monitor what you say to your friend for fear she will repeat it to others? Without trust, there is little room for a friendship to flourish. You will never be yourself around her if you feel a need to self-regulate what you share.

That's a lot to think about. Obviously, a **perfect friend** doesn't exist! But consider this.

In life, why not seek out relationships that make you feel happy?

Surely, life is far too short to spend it in the company of people who quite frankly leave you feeling a little cold, hurt or frustrated inside?

The questions in this chapter are long and extensive. You might think the expectations are huge and unrealistic. But we must remember that no one in this universe is perfect. No perfect friend exists. No perfect person exists in this world. Just like when looking for a life partner – he or she will not be perfect.

Your life partner will have flaws, just like you and I do. However, we hang around as the majority of the time your partner makes you feel happy and loved. It's really all about balance. It's the same with friends.

A good and healthy friend (just like a life partner) will exhibit *most* of these positive qualities, *most* of the time and without it being *too* difficult for her.

When a person is emotionally secure and content, he or she will exhibit an impressive array of positive behaviours. The behaviours will not be particularly challenging to 'keep up'; these people allow the positivity to naturally flow into your life. It is truly magical. They actively want to enhance your life and see your beautiful smile.

We have the power to choose our friendships in life. We would feel unhappy if our life partners did not support and love us, if they ignored us or judged us. Surely, we should insist our friendships (the people who are very close to us, the people we choose to spend our free time with) are also emotionally healthy.

We can choose our own path. A healthier, happier path. There is no need to play the games. We'll never learn the rules anyway. Every time you grasp the rules and think you are on top of female friendships – these women will simply change the rules!

***

Let's pause for a moment and consider this:

Friendship is like buying a cheap and nasty red wine. It doesn't matter what amazing tapas you serve with the wine or what funky glass you use – the nasty wine will leave a horrible taste in your mouth, it will give you a terrible hangover or a stain on your carpet.

You can't fake it; you can't cover up your feelings forever. If the friendship does not taste nice, you will always be pretending to drink it all up, when deep down you would like to spit it out and drink something nicer.

The fundamental truth is this - we must stop panic buying. Take your time and consider your options. Ask yourself the above questions. There is no rush to fill your life with people. Take your time and choose wisely.

Before you emotionally invest yourself and devote yourself to a friend, it pays to hold back a little and be sure this is a healthy friendship that deserves your time and energy. As we have seen, not all friendships are healthy or good for us. Your emotional well-being and happiness depends on healthy friendships.

Don't get caught out. Encourage the positive, be aware and if necessary, let go of the negative women. Life is too short to have apathetic, negative or unsatisfactory friendships.

Your mental health and personal happiness depends on your ability to see through the bullshit. Your well-being depends on your ability to read people's motivations. Your personal contentment depends on your ability to seek out the positive women and weed out the negative women.

Consider this. Most women take more time to decide on what car or house to buy. Most women are well-versed about taking their time with romantic relationships. Only fools rush in and although not always possible, most of the time we are cautious and try to take heed of this advice.

But with friends, the very people who we allow into our deepest, darkest inner circle - we can often be too relaxed. We often mistakenly believe a friend won't or can't hurt us. We think we are in control, but often we minimise the influence our friends can have on our individual happiness. Often we can let anyone and everyone into our life. There is little consideration about how this friend makes us feel, how they behave, how they encourage us to behave.

It is too easy to allow anyone and everyone into your life. While this carefree and open-minded approach will give you variety, spice and excitement, it could also bring you women who behave badly.

It is easy to invite the negative women into your life when you are emotionally vulnerable. Often when we are going through a big life change – like a new career, a new country or a new baby – we are incredibly vulnerable. Often we are so preoccupied with our big change, we let negative people in. We are not quite ourselves; perhaps we are not so confident or feel a little out of our depth.

We become an easy target for negative women to dig in their heels. They can blind us with promises of security. They are available and we are available and we mistakenly believe there is a healthy connection. Ask yourself, if you are single and another person you know is single – that does not automatically mean that you are now together. You have a *choice* about who you have relationships with!

As we have seen, negative women can be experts at hiding their dark side. They sparkle and shine, and only show you their most appealing side. They manipulate you, influence you and encourage you to believe they are a friend. Without you even knowing it, they have immense power over you. You have played into their hands and you didn't even know it.

Don't let this happen to you. Listen to your instincts. If someone is too good to be true – they most likely are! No woman on this planet is perfect. We all have many flaws.

If a woman has her friendship presented and packaged perfectly with a bow on top – be very wary. No friendship and no person can be perfect. She lives in a warped reality and she's hoping you can't resist buying her gift. She's hoping you won't notice her toxic reality.

With this book in your hands, you *will* notice her toxic reality. You know the truth about what can go on. You know what can happen between women.

***

But how on earth can you protect yourself?

To be honest, we can never be bulletproof. Sometimes you may still get hurt and fooled. But there is a clever way of protecting yourself from these toxic women. There is a way of minimising your risk of being hurt. I call it using your **emotional filter**.

You have the power to filter who you allow into your own life. Every time you meet a new person, consider if you actually want this person to be a friend. You can ask yourself if this person makes you feel comfortable, happy, relaxed? Or does this person make you feel uneasy, nervous, reserved? Do you have a good feeling about this person? Does she make you feel valued, acknowledged, respected?

There is a reason why we have two ears and one mouth. In order to emotionally filter – we must be patient and listen more. Instead of trying to impress, instead of trying to share funny stories, and instead of trying to be heard and understood – we must take a step back and listen. *We must listen more to a person than we talk to them.*

If we listen carefully to them, then we can emotionally filter out the people who are talking in a way that disturbs our values, morals and principles. If we chat, chat, chat about our own life and go on and on about what we think, what we believe and how we feel – we will never really know a person until it is too late and we are in too deep.

We have shared so much, gave so much of ourselves and the person has soaked it all up. But we have not really listened to them and still we do not know the person. We think we know the person, but how can we when we have rarely paid attention to their words or actions. We have been too busy talking about ourselves and ensuring they love us. We have been too busy holding the stage and ensuring they are listening to us. We have ignored our instincts. We may have ignored their curious actions, peculiar choice of words or strange questions. We are flattered that someone listens and so we talk and talk and talk. We prattle on but rarely listen to them.

Furthermore, we rarely consider the interesting notion that a person's character often echoes the questions they ask us. She asks questions that keep you talking and some may seem invasive or surprise you, but to her – it is important 'dirt' on you. She needs more and more information on you. She has an extensive character profile on you and you can barely describe who she is.

Which leads us to – you have the power to filter what you share with people. If you're anything like me, you will have been an open book. I used to be this way, too. I was far too open and accepting. I wanted to share my stories with people. I wanted people to know me, understand me. Sadly, this is not always a wise move. Some women will hold your hand, but really they are judging you; some will repeat your deepest darkest secrets.

After many years of being 'a sharer' and lacking the filter gene, I have concluded that it is wiser to filter what you share, even with the people who you have allowed into your inner sanction. People do not need to know every little thought and feeling you have. People do not need to know every detail of your past, present or future.

Let people make their own minds up about you, live your own life and let them live their own life. The real friends will love you no matter what and understand you. They will know you have good intentions. There is little point in trying to convince new people of your character. Only share what you want to share. Take a man's approach and only share when you feel you truly know a person; even then you may not want to share too much. That is your choice. You can decide.

Don't allow any woman to badger you into sharing just because it's what women do – it's how we bond! We do share a lot more; we are much more intimate with each other. But you can take a step back and be more cautious.

You can protect yourself by filtering who is in your life and what you share about yourself. Remember, listen more with those two ears and talk a little less. Listen, listen, listen to what you hear. If you talk, talk, talk – you'll miss the clues.

***

One last little insight that I hope will help.

Relationships cannot be built on weakness. We cannot build our relationships on jealousy, insecurity or unhappiness.

We may think we can; we may think we have met a person who thinks like us and how lovely it is that they agree with us and listen to us. But if each person contributes a bag of jealousy and another contributes a bag of insecurity, then pretty soon you will have foundations that are unsteady.

If two people build a relationship and each contributes their own dose of personal unhappiness, what do you have? A relationship built on weakness. A relationship that needs more unhappiness, more bitterness to fester and grow. Like an ugly monster, the relationship will perish if it's not fed with more negative fuel.

If one person suddenly wakes up and decides to bring in some positivity, then the relationship will be strained. There's not enough strength in the foundations.

This often happens when two women unite and bitch about a third woman. They unite thanks to their similar hostility towards a woman. They delight in bitching about her and become closer with each bitching session. Their relationship is built on negative emotions. It is not built from love or bliss or kindness. I am sure you can figure out – it won't be long until they begin to attack each other.

Relationships must be built on strength. People must bring some contentment, some love, some compassion and some respect to the relationship. Without these elements, the relationship will be on borrowed time.

Always build your relationships on strength. No healthy or long-term friendships can foster from a united hate or a shared bitterness.

No healthy relationships can be built out of gossiping or bitching.

Uniting with each other must come from love, trust and respect for each other and for other people and not from a shared hatred.

I sincerely hope that as time goes on, you will need to refer to this book less and less. I hope as time passes you will engage in only healthy female friendships.

I wish you much luck and love as you embark on this journey. I feel confident, armed with this book's advice and insights, you will allow only positive and healthy female friends into your precious life.

The Ridiculous Behaviours

I couldn't write this book without highlighting some of the *more* ridiculous behaviours that I have witnessed time and time again. Perhaps you'll recognise them, too? Put on the kettle and grab yourself a cuppa. These behaviours will make you chuckle or scream!

Have you ever gone out for a meal with a group of women? Once the bill arrives this is what happens.

Some or all of the women will be secretly calculating in their heads what their *own individual bill* is.

I had the salad; she had the chicken pasta and an extra wine, so I'll be paying a lot less.

Or they shamelessly bash away at the calculator downloaded to their smart phone. I wish I was joking.

Or picture this - they jump up and ask the waiter to separate the bill as everybody wishes to pay individually.

They might even make their way to the cash point and *only pay their own bill*. You are still sipping the last of your coffee and nibbling the chocolate mint; she's standing at the cash point educating the waiting staff on what she is paying for. It sure won't be your desert, sweetie!

Call me crazy, but are any of the above behaviours a generous and friendly way to end a meal?

You have just sat for an hour or more, no doubt emotionally supporting each other, hugging in the toilet, laughing together, bonding, sharing your deepest secrets, scheduling your next meet up, but you can't help but notice that she looks after herself first and is perhaps too quick to pay her own bill or grab her change.

Contrast these experiences to eating with a group of men. Nobody really looks at the bill *too* closely. They have a general idea of how much they contributed to the final bill. Everybody chucks in *equal* amounts of cash. There is no debate, no tapping away on a calculator, and rushing off to pay their own bill. They have not said much to each other that is meaningful or deep, but they know it is rude to plonk a calculator on the table and they know it is bloody annoying for the waiter to have to split a bill for a group of close friends.

It is man law to also ensure that the Birthday Boy does not put his hand in his pocket on a meal out. I find this practice reassuring but somewhat depressing simply because of my own experiences.

On my 20th birthday meal out with a group of 12 females, and with not an ounce of awkwardness, I was asked,

"So is your dad paying for this meal, Alana?"

Some of my university *friends* had only come along at the prospect of a free meal on my birthday. My dad wasn't paying for them. I, of course, was expected to pay my own bill. Happy Birthday!

And yet, despite their inherent tightness, women hand me beautifully decorated little gift bags in shades of pastel and cards that tell me how special I am. Something doesn't quite add up. Hey, don't get me wrong, I love the scented candles, but maybe a little more generosity after a shared meal is needed. Ladies, *please* put away the calculator.

***

Women are also fun to watch in shops. Make no mistake about it; the shop assistants of big super stores will always prefer to work in the men's department. And there's a reason why! I worked in a ladies fashion shop when I was a student and I spent the majority of my time picking up clothes from the floor and placing items back to their correct location. Have you ever noticed how messy women are in shops? I'd go visit a friend in the men's department and notice how tidy it was in comparison. The assistants can be bored stiff some days as most men are militant about returning their clothes to the rack. Rarely is an item ever left on the floor. It is quite amazing to witness the difference.

Women can also be pushy customers. I've been pushed out of the way by a woman desperate to see a sales rack. I also remember having to pick up all the dresses she had dropped on the shop floor. Good grief! It was enough to drive any retail assistant temporary insane.

Ever witnessed a female in the supermarket? I've lost count of the number of times I have had to move a trolley or been hemmed in because a woman's left her trolley slap bang in the middle of a food aisle. If I say, *"Excuse me,"* I will usually get a tut or a glare from her because I have *inconvenienced her*. If her husband is beside her, he will usually notice first, apologise and move the trolley out of my path as quick as he can. She'll just look at me and let her husband deal with it. Isn't it amazing? Like some people can become ignorant pigs behind a wheel of a car, some women lose all basic manners in the supermarket. This is her aisle, you can just wait! Well I do, rather a lot of the time. I just stand there like a prat and wait patiently.

***

But wait. Let's consider the most bizarre behaviour of all.

The most irritating and ridiculous behaviour of all is women who pretend to love you when they actually don't rate you at all. They will come to your party, compliment you, smile at you, bring you a gift and hug you goodbye. They'll leave and you think they are a friend. But they don't actually like you. They are only being *'nice'*.

Can anyone explain this strange phenomenon? Why do women come to your home for a Sunday BBQ and hug you good bye when they don't like you? Why do women wish you good luck at your leaving do, bring you flowers and kiss you, when they are glad to see the back of you? Why do women invite you out for drinks, but spend most the evening talking to anyone else but you? Hmm, it certainly is a curious approach. This pretending to be nice, pretending to adore a person when deep down they actually dream of gorging your eyes out with a blunt pencil. It's disturbing.

Wouldn't it be easier to just be honest and stop pretending? Wouldn't it be wonderful if some women could stop all this indirect bullshit and just be real? I want to hit these women hard over the head with a club and tell them to stop *'playing nice'* and just be a real human being.

In Conclusion

Why attack other women; aren't we meant to be sisters in this great big world?

I hope I have left you with much to ponder. From the ridiculous, zealous calculating of a bill to the cruel power games or the earnest bitching, I've showed you the challenges we must face when dealing with women in our life. And, of course, let's not forget the intense expectations heavily weighed on our heads. I hope I have helped to awaken you to the realities of being around women.

It isn't an easy option to tick 'female' on the application form of life. We are tough on each other and even tougher on ourselves.

We women have fought long and hard to be listened to. We've come *together* and fought against discrimination, oppression and patriarchy. We are *still* fighting today for our reproductive rights, for equal pay, for affordable child care. We continue to fight against sexual harassment and to end the horrors of domestic violence. It is not over yet, but we ought to be proud of what we have achieved so far in history. We have accomplished much in our cosy Western bubble (although we still have important problems to solve), and today, all over the world, developing countries are also fighting for their own equality rights. This is amazing. Feminism is a powerful force; it is relevant and constantly evolving as society pushes forward.

However, we must ask a rather irksome question - have women become so focused on creating and maintaining equality in the greater outside world that we have forgotten about the importance of ensuring equality *between* the women in our daily life? Feminism assumes that women are the victims of political, economic and social injustices. I would agree; we are indeed the victims of a patriarchal world. The world is *still* largely male dominated and women still earn less income than their male work colleagues. Women *still* fear for their safety. Women have a much higher risk of abuse and sexual violence. So why do we sometimes victimise other women and give other women such a torrid time? Why aren't we gentler on other women? Have women not endured enough already? Why don't we protect each other more? Why do we turn on each other with ease?

We must stop fighting with *each other*. We have become so used to pushing up against oppression that we habitually persecute other women. We have become so used to being attacked; we are ready to fight, but sometimes we fight with each other. In order to feel safe in this world, women must treat other women as allies, as loyal friends and not as competition. Attacking each other serves us no positive purpose. Too many women try to assert their power over other women instead of nurturing other women. We need to respect each other and stop trying to gain power over each other. We must stop being the righteous chorus who believe we have the right to judge other women. Why do women often sit on a haughty perch? Why do we measure other women by a set of strict social rules? Why do we feel the need to scrutinise other women? Perfection does not exist within human beings, so why do women harass and besiege other women? Why do women persistently hound and badger other females with the nonsensical notion of flawlessness?

I could give you endless examples to support my concerns. But I will stick to one that jumps out. Picture this – a young mother who happens to be a celebrity in Australia; she has the *nerve* to walk while she breastfeeds her new baby. Milk on the go. An alarming chorus of women bleat at this action. Stricken with horror, women tap away furiously on social media websites. *How could she do this? What a terrible mother! Poor child! She should be sitting down and looking into her baby's eyes. That's not how a mother behaves.* Cue a celebrity mother close to a nervous breakdown and crying herself to sleep believing she is a useless mother. It's a horrible reality of women; we are thorny to each other. Like a swarm of pesky mosquitos, women can pursue relentlessly.

Have feminists tried to ignore and minimise the negative reality of human nature to promote their ideologies? Have we forgotten that women are humans with profound short comings just like men? The multiple ideologies of Feminism are necessary but ultimately unrealistic because utopia can't possibly exist in this world. We can fight for fairness and demand that men treat us fairly, but women are just as likely to be unfair and inhumane towards each other. We can be our own hardest critics, our own worst enemy. Women hurt and oppress each other and throughout history, women have helped aid men to victimise women. Women will exploit other women; we are not all honourable friends to each other. Women are humans and humans will sometimes behave badly. It is too easy, we are easy targets, and we know each other's weak points. We lash out, ridicule, bully, criticise, and judge each other. It is easier for women to attack each other than to fight against society or men. The easiest target to hit with our societal frustration is women.

The best solution to happiness within groups of women is to fight for a fairer future but also to work together. Our urge to attack other women is the biggest threat that faces feminism today. Pointing out that a friend has put on some weight post-baby, being jealous of a friend's personal goal, bitching about a friend's parenting tactics or competing with other women to have the sexiest bum at the gym is offensive to the prior women who fought for our equal rights.

Let's not let the ridiculous pressures of our modern world get in the way of our relationships with other women. Finding faults in each other, being tough on each other and trying to assert dominance will only ensure that women continue to behave badly around one another. We will struggle to unite and care for other women if we are preoccupied with pointing the finger at a woman who doesn't meet our society's strict moral code of how a mother should behave or how a woman should look.

We must stop wanting to pull the trigger on each other and throw down our toxic guns. Holding each other to ransom only wounds and torments all women. Who really benefits? Why attack our best ally? The gender who understands our daily struggles? We don't need to fight with *each other,* we have enough *already* to fight for. Respecting our individual differences is a step in the right direction. Being kinder to one another is essential.

Thank You

It's not easy to write a book with three kids buzzing around, but I had to grab my chances. Isn't that life? We all have to grab our chances. I could not have achieved this without the loving support of my family.

Thank you to my husband, Michael, who took time out of his days at work to send me emails and encouraged me to keep writing. Thanks, honey, for telling me I *have* to write.

Thank you to my mum and dad who asked me constantly how I was getting on with my book. Dad, sorry if you can't quite retire after this book goes to print. Mum, I love how you believe in me.

Thank you to my beautiful boys, Ethan, Arden and Laike. *"Come on, Mum! Get on with your book, we want the computer back!"*

Thank you to my beautiful puppy, Evie, my loyal companion. She would lick my toes and whine for play time in the garden. It all helped me to clear my head. She would lie at my feet for hours, sleeping peacefully as I typed.

And one last thing, I want to say thank you to the females who inspired me to write this book.

Thank you to all the women in my life, past and present, who have taught me important life lessons.

To every female who has gossiped about me, to the angry girls who cornered me in the school toilets, pushed me around, shouted expletives constantly and to the girls who wrote hideous lies about me on the school walls. Thanks!

To every female who has ever abused me, to those who have rejected me, judged me and ignored me without understanding who I am inside or the pain I was enduring in my life. Thanks!

To every female who wielded power over me – for the rumours and lies you spread, the ridicule, the demands, the bullying, the harassment, the persecution, the humiliation, the jealousy, the disloyalty, the disgust, the desperation, the rage, the fear. Thanks!

Thank you for teaching me the importance of integrity, compassion and empathy. I wouldn't be who I am without the lessons!

It is through pain, through discrimination, through bullying, through anger, through your mistakes and my mistakes that I have discovered what happiness is. I'm still here. I'm a living, breathing, loving woman. You didn't crush my spirit. I wouldn't let you. Hello, future!

About Alana Munro

Email me at:alanamunroauthor@gmail.com

Alana lives in the hot Pilbara Desert which is at the top end of Western Australia (she's actually a Scottish lass) with her husband, three gorgeous sons and their adorable puppy. It is a land of red dust and iron ore. The sea is full of sharks and monster crabs. The sky has a blazing sun every day. It's a little bit different from Scotland.

This is Alana's debut book and she hopes to write more in the future. If you want to express interest in this book or future book projects, simply drop Alana an email and she'll reply for sure. If you want to share any of your personal experiences about women, please drop Alana an email. She'd love to hear from you.

***

***

8287893R00059

Printed in Great Britain
by Amazon.co.uk, Ltd.,
Marston Gate.